Feathered
Friends

Feathered Friends

The 1983 Childcraft Annual

An annual supplement to
Childcraft – The How and Why Library

World Book, Inc.

a Scott Fetzer company

Chicago London Sydney Toronto

Acknowledgments

The publishers of *Childcraft—The How and Why
Library* gratefully acknowledge the courtesy of the
following publishers, agencies, authors, and organizations for permission to use copyrighted material
in this volume. Full illustration acknowledgments
appear on page 296.

Nature Conservancy: Excerpt from "There Once
Was a Puffin," by Florence Jaques, used by
permission of the Nature Conservancy.

**photographs on
preceding pages**

page 1: a puffin in flight
pages 2–3: a Black Swan
and cygnets

Contents

Preface

Whether you live at the edge of a desert or in the middle of a crowded city, you probably see some birds every day. But most of us don't pay much attention to birds, and don't know much about them. And that's too bad, because birds are really marvelous creatures. They do many interesting—and sometimes amazing—things.

Birds are also very important to the balance of nature. By eating insects, many birds help keep insects from becoming too numerous. And some kinds of birds help plants reproduce by carrying pollen from one plant to another or by spreading their seeds.

This book shows you the many different ways of life of birds. Some of the birds you will read about will be those that you often see. You'll find that when you know a little about a bird's way of life, it's a lot of fun to look for that bird. Perhaps you will see it do some of the things you've read about. Then you'll begin to see how interesting bird watching can be!

There are more than eight thousand different kinds of birds—so many it just isn't possible to have all of them in a book this size. So, if one of your favorites has been left out, we're sorry. We just couldn't fit them all in!

What Is a Bird?

Cactus Wren

Feathers are what make a bird able to fly. They form its wings and tail.

photographs on pages 8–9

White Pelicans in flight, and a Red and Green Macaw

Feathers make a bird

What makes a bird different from every other kind of creature? The answer is just one word—*feathers*. Birds are the only creatures that have feathers. Feathers are what make a bird a bird!

Feathers do a number of things for a bird. For one thing, they make it possible for most birds to fly. The feathers on a bird's "arms" form wings that are stiff, tough, and wide, but very, very light. The wings lift the bird up and, as the bird flaps its wings, some of the wing feathers twist back and forth, pushing the bird through the air.

Feathers also keep a bird warm. The feathers on a bird's body form a tight coat that keeps body heat in, even in cold weather.

Some birds have waterproof feathers. These birds can swim and dive without getting waterlogged and sinking.

The colors of feathers can be important, too. Bright colors help some birds to attract a mate. Other colors are for protection. If the colors make the birds hard to see, hungry enemies won't notice them. When a Whippoorwill crouches on the ground in a woods, its feathers blend into the background. The bird looks much like a pile of leaves, a rock, or part of an old log.

A feather isn't a live part of a bird, like its skin. You could cut a feather in two and it wouldn't bleed, or hurt the bird, any more than your hair bleeds or hurts you when it's cut. In fact, birds turn their feathers in for a new set at least once a year! Slowly, a few at a time, old feathers fall out and new ones grow in. This is called molting (MOHLT ihng), and usually takes from four to six weeks.

Willow Ptarmigan
The colors of their feathers make it easy for some kinds of birds to hide.

Wings are for flying —sometimes

All birds have wings. Wings, of course, are for flying, and most birds can fly. Many kinds of birds are good flyers. Other kinds really can't fly very well. There are some birds that can fly, but don't like to and seldom do. And there

Wandering Albatross

An albatross has long wings that enable it to soar on the wind for hours at a time.

are some birds that can't fly at all, even though they have wings.

The wings of most birds look rather thick and heavy. But a bird's wings are really quite thin and very light. They are nothing but a few slim bones covered with thin skin that has feathers attached.

Bird wings aren't all the same. Different kinds of birds have different kinds of wings. The kind of wings a bird has depends a lot upon the bird's way of life.

The way of life of a Wandering Albatross is to soar far out over the sea, for months at a time. An albatross has very long, pointed wings. When these are stretched straight out, the wind lifts the bird up and carries it along like a kite. A Wandering Albatross can soar on the wind for hours without once having to flap its wings. This slow, gliding way of flying helps the bird find food—small creatures floating or swimming on the surface of the water.

Chimney Swift
A Chimney Swift's wings are shaped for fast flying and very quick turns.

A Chimney Swift also spends most of its life flying. But a swift's food is flying insects, which it catches in the air. So, a swift has to be able to fly fast and make quick, sharp turns. It has narrow, tapered wings. By flapping its wings fast and hard, a swift can move at terrific speed and change direction quickly.

A penguin spends much of its life in the sea. This bird is a very fine swimmer, but it

Ring-Necked Pheasant

A pheasant's wings are good for a quick take-off.

cannot fly. In the water, a penguin uses its wings as paddles to swim after fish and other sea creatures that it eats.

The Ring-Necked Pheasant (FEHZ uhnt) spends most of its life on the ground. It walks about looking for seeds, berries, and insects to eat. It is often in danger, for a fox or other animal may suddenly rush at it. However, a pheasant has broad, rounded wings that enable it to take off quickly. It can shoot up into the air and escape. But it can't fly very high or far on such wings, and soon glides back down to the ground.

An ostrich (AW strihch) spends *all* its life on the ground. Its wings look like big fans, but they cannot lift the ostrich's big, heavy body

Emperor Penguins

Penguins use their wings for swimming. These birds can't fly.

ostriches

Ostriches often hold out their wings for balance as they run. They cannot fly.

into the air. An ostrich cannot fly, but it can run like the wind. When it runs, it often holds its wings straight out to help it keep its balance.

The little New Zealand bird called a kiwi (KEE wee) also spends all its life on the ground. Its tiny, useless wings are hidden by shaggy feathers. Kiwis cannot fly and they don't have to run because they have no enemies where they live. So, kiwis don't use their wings for anything.

Some birds use their wings for flying and some use them for swimming. Other birds use their wings to help them run, or even to help them walk. Some birds use their wings for fighting! And a few birds don't use their wings for anything at all.

A bill for every need

All birds have a bill. The upper and lower parts of the bill are parts of a bird's jaws. Your jaws have teeth in them, but there are no teeth in a bird's bill. You use your jaws mostly for chewing. But a bird's bill usually forms a very special tool that the bird uses for getting its food.

For many birds such as sparrows, crows, and starlings, a bill is a pair of "tweezers." It is used to pick up seeds, insects, and other things. Other kinds of birds need food that can't be picked up. So, they have bills that work like chisels, straws, scoops, spears, or other kinds of tools, depending on what the birds eat.

Blue Jay

Many birds have bills that are like tweezers. The bills are good for picking up and holding things.

nutcracker bill
The large, strong bill of a grosbeak can crack open tough seeds.

hooked bill
A bird of prey such as a falcon has a hooked bill for tearing up its food.

probing bill
A curlew's long, thin bill is just right for probing in mud or sand for worms, clams, snails, and insects.

chisel bill
A sapsucker's bill is like a chisel for cutting into wood to get food.

Woodpeckers and sapsuckers get their food out of the trunks and branches of trees. Most woodpeckers eat insects that live in tree trunks. Sapsuckers eat the sugary sap that flows through a tree's trunk and branches. To get their food, these birds must be able to dig holes in a tree. Their bills are like chisels. By hammering their bills against trees, the birds gouge out wood chips and make holes.

Nectar, the sweet syrup that lies deep inside many flowers, is the main food of most hummingbirds. A hummingbird's long, thin bill is like a tube that can reach down into a flower to get at the nectar. The bird's tongue is a long sipper, longer than the bill itself. A hummingbird pokes its bill into a flower. Then it stretches its tongue through the bill to suck up nectar and small insects.

Curlews (KUR looz), snipes (snypes), woodcocks, and several other kinds of birds also have long, thin bills. But their food is mainly worms or other creatures that live in the ground. These birds push their long bills down into soft earth, mud, or sand to feel for the creatures they eat.

Parrots, grosbeaks, and some other birds that eat hard seeds have short, stout bills that are like powerful nutcrackers. A Hawfinch has a sturdy bill that can even crack open the stony-hard seed of an olive.

Some birds are known as birds of prey, because they hunt and eat, or prey upon, other birds and small animals. Hawks, owls, and falcons are all birds of prey. You can tell a bird of prey by the upper part of its bill, which curves down to form a sharp hook. The bird uses this hook to tear meat from the bodies of the creatures it kills.

Albatrosses, frigate birds, and several other kinds of sea birds also have hooked bills. These birds get most of their food by grabbing

tube bill
The Broad-Tailed Hummingbird's bill is a long tube that can reach into a flower.

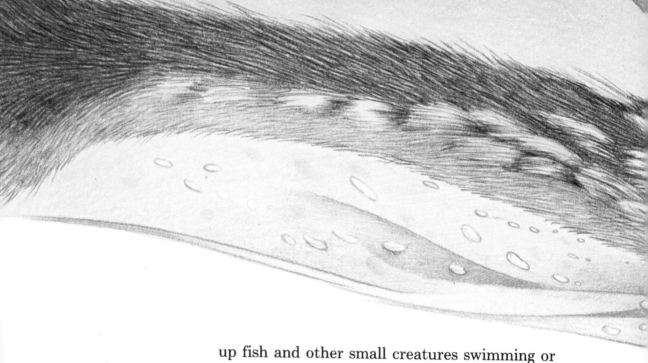

up fish and other small creatures swimming or
floating near the surface of the water. The
hook makes it easier for the birds to catch
their prey.

Herons, kingfishers, and anhingas (an HIHNG
guhz) have bills that look like spears. And
they often use their bills as spears. They stab
the sharp point into fish so that the fish can
be lifted out of the water.

Many birds use their bill for other things
beside getting food. Most birds use their bill
to smooth their feathers, which is called
preening. Some birds have a gland near the
base of the tail that gives off an oily liquid
when it's rubbed. A bird rubs its bill on the
gland to coat it with oil. Then it rubs the bill
through its feathers to make them smooth and
glossy. Other birds clean themselves with a
powder that comes from special feathers.

Most birds that make nests use their bill to
carry building materials—blobs of mud, bits of

spear bill

An anhinga uses its
bill as a spear to kill
fish and other animals.

grass, small twigs, and other things. They also
use their bill to push and pull materials into
the right shape for the nest. A female
tailorbird uses her long, pointed bill as a
needle to sew a leaf together for her nest! For
thread, she uses thin plant stems or silk from
a spider web or cocoon.

There are a great many different kinds of
bird bills. No matter how strange a bill may
look, you can be sure the bird has some
way—probably several ways—of putting its
bill to good use.

22

House Sparrow
Sparrows and all other
perching birds can
easily wrap their toes
around slim perches
like twigs and wires.

All kinds of feet

All people have the same kind of feet, but all
birds don't. The feet of one kind of bird can
be very different from those of another kind of
bird. Birds need the kind of feet that are
suited to their way of life.

Many birds, such as robins, sparrows, and
jays, spend a great deal of time in the
branches of trees and bushes. These birds
have feet that enable them to stand on very
thin twigs and even on telephone wires.

Because they can use such narrow perches, they are known as perching birds.

The feet of most perching birds have three toes that point forward and one toe that points backward. When the birds perch, they use the front toes like fingers and the back toe like a thumb. They curl their toes around a twig like you curl your thumb and fingers around a rake handle. A built-in locking device pulls the toes into a fist and gives a perching bird such a tight grip that it won't fall off even when it goes to sleep.

Woodpeckers spend most of their time in trees, but they aren't perching birds. Their feet have two toes that point forward and two that point back—like an X. The toes have sharp little curved claws. With these feet, a woodpecker can take little hops straight up the side of a tree, digging its toes in at each hop. Being able to hold on and to move up the side of a tree this way is very important to the woodpecker for getting food.

Many birds, such as grouse and turkeys, that stay mostly on the ground and get their food there, have feet shaped like the feet of perching birds. But instead of having long, curved claws like perching birds, they have claws that are short and blunt. These ground birds use their claws like rakes. They scratch the ground to turn up seeds and insects to eat.

Many kinds of birds spend most of their time in water. Some of these, such as ducks

24

Gila Woodpecker

A woodpecker's feet
are shaped to help it
scoot up a tree trunk.

Bald Eagle

A bird of prey has sharp, curved
talons, or claws, on its feet.
These talons are tools for killing
or holding the bird's prey.

Western Grebes
Many swimming birds have toes like little paddles. This helps them swim.

and swans, have webbed feet that are like swim fins. Others, such as phalaropes (FAL uh rohps) and grebes (greebz), have toes with flaps of skin on them. These flaps of skin turn the toes into little paddles. Feet like this make these birds good swimmers.

The feet of birds of prey, such as falcons and hawks, are deadly weapons used for hunting. Their feet have strong toes with large, sharp, curved claws. A bird of prey uses its feet to grab the small animals or birds that are its food. Its grip is very powerful, and its sharp claws stab into its prey, usually causing instant death.

These are only a few of the many different kinds of bird feet. But, as you can see, a bird's feet are suited to the bird's way of life.

Yellow-Bellied Sapsucker

Sapsuckers, flickers, and woodpeckers use their tail as a prop when clinging to a tree trunk.

A tale of tails

The *real* tail of a bird is usually just a small stub. But there may be anywhere from four to forty large feathers attached to this stub. When people talk of a bird's tail, they really mean tail feathers.

Most birds that are good fliers use their tail feathers to help balance and steer themselves. They spread the feathers out to form a fan. By moving their tail, they can change direction.

Many birds also use their tail as a brake. When a duck comes sailing down to alight in water, it spreads its tail and points it downward. The air pushes into this fan of feathers and causes the bird to slow down.

Some birds use their tail as a support. A woodpecker usually clings to the side of a tree trunk with its head pointed up and its tail pointed down. It holds its tail at an angle, so that the end of the tail is propped against the tree. This support helps keep the bird from sliding down. Swifts and some other birds also use their tails this way.

For some birds, a tail is a very special ornament. You may have seen a picture of a male turkey with his tail spread out like a big fan. But a turkey's tail doesn't always look that way. A male turkey only spreads his tail out during the mating season. At the same time, he puffs up his whole body, so he looks

Indian Peacock

The male peafowl, or peacock (above), is the national bird of India. The male lyrebird (right) is one of the marvels of Australia. Both birds spread their beautiful tails to attract the attention of females at mating time.

Superb Lyrebird

much bigger and more colorful. He does these things to attract females and show his power to other males.

A number of other birds also have fancy tails for attracting mates. The tail of the male lyrebird of Australia looks like the kind of old-fashioned harp called a lyre. The best-known bird tail of all is the huge tail of the peafowl, or peacock, which looks as if it is covered with strange, glowing eyes!

Bird calls and songs

A crow, flapping across a meadow, screeches a shrill *caw!* In the distance, another crow answers. *Caw!* A bright-red male Cardinal, sitting on a tree branch, bursts into song—*wheet-chur, wheet-chur, wheet, wheet, wheet!* A Chaffinch in a woods whistles a long, shrill *seeeeet!*

Do any of these sounds *mean* anything? Yes, they do. Birds do have a kind of "language"! Almost every sound they make has a meaning.

The tunes that most songbirds sing in the springtime have two meanings. Most of this singing is done by the males. Their songs are actually *warnings* to other males. Each male bird has a territory that he has picked out, and his song warns other males to stay out of it or he'll fight them! But at the same time, the song is also an invitation to females. Early in the nesting season, it invites any female who hears it to be the male's mate.

Most of the other sounds that birds make are just single noises rather than songs. But these noises, too, usually have meaning.

Many birds have a call that means "danger." If one of these birds sees a hawk gliding overhead, or a fox slinking through the underbrush, it will give its danger call. This warns other birds, so they can hide or flee. Each different kind of bird usually has its own "language," but many birds can often understand another bird's danger call.

Many kinds of birds that live in groups, or flocks, have a call that means "Here I am." When they are looking for food on the ground, or flying at night, the birds in a flock may not be able to see one another. So, from time to time, each bird will give the "here I am" call. This lets each bird know that others are nearby, and helps keep any of the birds from getting separated from the rest of the flock or lost.

Birds also have calls that mean "I've found food," "I'm in trouble," and "Come here." Many baby birds make loud noises that just mean, "I'm hungry! Please feed me!"

Nurseries for baby birds

At a certain time of year, usually in the spring, a bird's instincts make it want to mate and have babies. This is when most birds make their nest. The nest is where the female bird lays her eggs after she has mated. It is a "nursery," where baby birds are cared for until they can look after themselves. Some nests are built only by female birds, some only by males. Some nests are built by both birds.

Different kinds of birds make different kinds of nests. Many kinds of birds make nests in trees. Some of these nests are platforms of twigs piled together. Others are like bowls, made of mud and grass. And some are hanging pouches, made of twigs and grass woven together. Woodpecker nests are holes in tree trunks. The birds bore these holes with their bills.

Many birds make their nest on the ground. Some make round nests of grass and weeds. Some make big, bulky domes of leaves and tree bark. Some birds dig holes in the ground, and lay their eggs in the holes. Some birds just take over old holes that were dug by other animals.

Some water birds build nests on the water. These nests are floating rafts made of water plants piled together.

Some birds don't bother to make a nest. They lay their eggs on cliff ledges high above

The nest of a Ruby-Throated Hummingbird is a deep cup made of plant fuzz, spider webs, and moss fastened to a small tree branch.

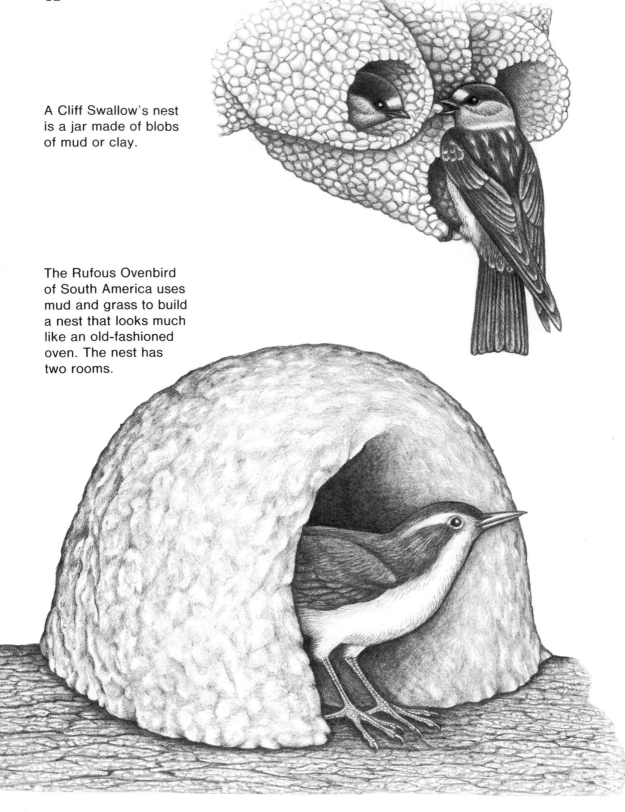

A Cliff Swallow's nest is a jar made of blobs of mud or clay.

The Rufous Ovenbird of South America uses mud and grass to build a nest that looks much like an old-fashioned oven. The nest has two rooms.

The European Blackbird makes its nest of grass, paper, fur, and other odds and ends. The nest may be on a ledge, in the corner of a building, or in a tree or bush.

the ground, or above the surging sea. Some just lay their eggs on a sandy beach, or on the leaves that cover a forest floor.

There are a great many different kinds of bird nests. The kind of nest a bird makes depends a lot upon where and how it lives.

Bobwhite incubating eggs

Eggs must be kept warm in order to hatch. Many birds squat on their eggs to warm them. This is called incubation.

Eggs and baby birds

All baby birds come from eggs. When a mother bird lays an egg, it contains a golden-orange yolk, upon which is a tiny ring of living cells. The yolk is the food that will give the cells the energy to slowly grow into a baby bird.

But to live and grow, the little creature in the egg needs warmth. In most cases the mother bird crouches over the eggs to keep them warm with her body. Sometimes the father bird does this. Sometimes a mother and father take turns. This warming of the eggs is called incubation (ihn kyuh BAY shuhn).

Some bird eggs take less than two weeks to hatch. Other eggs, especially large ones, may take more than two months. As the weeks pass, the baby bird inside each egg changes and grows. Its yolk-food is slowly used up. Finally, the baby bird fills the whole inside of the egg. It begins to squirm.

Each baby bird has a sharp little spike on its bill. As the baby squirms and wiggles, the spike scrapes against the inside of the eggshell, making cracks and holes. As the baby pushes more and more, the egg begins to break open. After a time, the little bird forces its way out into the world.

A baby Herring Gull hatching from its egg.

**American Robin
and its young**

Some kinds of newborn birds have their eyes closed and do not have any feathers. Weak and helpless, they have to be fed by the parents.

Many baby birds are completely helpless when they hatch. Their eyes are closed, and they have no feathers. They are so weak they can barely move. Without their parents to bring them food and look after them, they would die. All perching birds, as well as woodpeckers and a number of other kinds, are like this when they hatch.

Because they have no feathers, these baby birds must be kept warm. The mother, or sometimes the father, warms the babies by crouching over them for a time and covering them with her wings. This is called brooding.

In time, the little birds get stronger. Their eyes open, and they begin to grow feathers. They no longer have to be brooded.

Depending on the kind of bird they are, they will be able to leave the nest in anywhere from a little more than a week to a month or more.

Other baby birds look quite different when they hatch. They come out of the egg with their eyes open and with a coat of soft feathers called *down*. They can walk almost at

ostrich and chicks

Some kinds of newborn birds can see and have soft feathers. Within hours, they are strong enough to run about and get their own food.

once. Some can even run within a few hours. Ducks, geese, and a number of other birds are like this when they hatch. They can take care of themselves almost at once.

But even though these kinds of baby birds aren't helpless, most of them still stay with their mother or father until they are grown. They, too, have to be brooded for a while, and taught how to get their food. Most important, they have to be protected from other animals.

Most kinds of birds are very good parents. Most birds take good care of their young until they are old enough to be on their own.

Canada Goose and goslings

Baby geese, ducks, and swans can swim as soon as they hatch.

Migrating Snow Geese, flying in a V formation, stand out against a bright blue sky.

The twice-a-year trip

Twice each year, in the spring and fall, millions of birds make a journey. They leave the part of the world where they have lived for perhaps half a year, and fly to another part for the rest of the year. Such a journey is called a migration (my GRAY shuhn), which means "moving from one place to another."

Birds always migrate to the same places every year—the places their ancestors have gone to for thousands of years. For some birds, this is a journey of only a few miles (kilometers). For others, it is a journey that covers thousands of miles (kilometers) and takes months. The birds seem to find their way by using the sun, or the moon and stars, as a compass!

40

Starlings gather in huge flocks when they are ready to migrate.

the greatest traveler

The Arctic Tern makes the longest migration of any bird—from the Arctic to the Antarctic and back. It flies about 11,000 miles (17,700 kilometers) each way.

Why do birds migrate? In many parts of the world, the food birds eat is scarce at certain times of the year. So, the birds migrate to a place where there is plenty. When fall comes to the northern part of the world, and insects begin to die off or go into hiding for the winter, many birds that eat insects must migrate. They fly to southern parts of the world, where the weather will be warm for the next six months or so, and there will be plenty of insects to eat.

Then, about six months later, the birds migrate again. They fly back north, where it is now spring, and food is becoming plentiful once more. It is a time when billions of insects are hatching out of their eggs.

It seems as if the birds are very smart to know when food will be running out, and to know when it is becoming plentiful. But, actually, the birds *don't* know. Certain changes that take place in their bodies in the spring and fall make them migrate. They really can't help themselves.

Some kinds of birds gather together and migrate in huge flocks. Other kinds make their journey alone. Some birds fly only at night when they migrate, and others fly only by day. Most birds don't fly steadily, but often stop to rest or find food.

A great many kinds of birds do not migrate. As long as a bird can find food and water where it is, it has no need to migrate.

Alike and different

A sparrow is much smaller than a crow, and it is brown while a crow is black. But in some ways the two are really very much alike. They have the same sort of feet, the same sort of bill, and their wings are much alike. This is because they're actually distant "cousins." They both belong to a group, or *order*, of birds that are all known as perching birds.

Water Birds with Four Webbed Toes

White Pelican

Blue-Faced Booby

Fowls

Ring-Necked Pheasant

Greater Prairie Chicken

Long-legged Wading Birds

Shoebill

Great White Heron

Birds of Prey That Hunt in the Daytime

White-Tailed Eagle

Birds of Prey That Hunt at Night

Screech Owl

Turkey Vulture

Barn Owl

However, a pelican doesn't look a bit like a crow or sparrow. It has different feet, a different bill, even a different-looking body. It isn't a perching bird. It belongs to a completely different order of birds.

Although we call all these winged creatures "birds," they're often very different from one another. There are twenty-eight different orders of birds. Some of the birds that belong to a few of the orders are shown here—so that you can see that while the birds in each order are much alike, they are quite different from those in every other order.

Birds of Town and City

The first sign of spring

It was a bright morning in early April. In a small woods, the last icy patches of winter snow were melting away. The lawns of a nearby town were fresh and green. Trees were beginning to bud.

A blur of orange and brown sailed through the air and alighted on the roof of a house. It was a plump bird with brown back and wings and orange-red breast—a male American Robin. The robin cocked a bright, beady eye toward the lawn to see if any earthworms were about. Then he opened his bill and sang.

"Cheerdilee, cheerdilee, cheerdilee!"

In the house next door, a little boy heard the song. He looked out of a window, saw the robin, and grinned. It was the first robin he'd seen this year—and that meant winter was over! Like many Americans, he knew that the first robin was a sure sign of spring.

photographs on pages 44–45

a flock of pigeons on a city street, and an American Robin

Within a few days, the male robin was joined by a female. Soon, she began to build a nest. She picked out a place among the branches of a large evergreen shrub that sprawled under the kitchen windows of a house. It was well hidden from any birds that might fly overhead, as well as from people that might pass by. It was also too high for a dog's curious nose to poke into, and in too hard a place for a cat to get at.

The female began by making a platform of twigs and grass on a branch. Then, bringing billfuls of grass and mud—and sometimes bits of string, cloth, or paper that she found on lawns and sidewalks—she built up the sides of the nest. The mud dried hard and held everything together.

When the sides and bottom were thick and firm, the robin brought billfuls of mud. She smeared the mud all over the inside of the nest. Then she squatted in the nest and turned around and around several times. This smoothed the mud and gave the inside of the nest a bowl shape. The robin then lined the inside of the nest with soft grass. Now, everything was ready.

Within a few days she had laid four pale-blue eggs in the bottom of the nest. She spent most of the next dozen days squatting upon the eggs to keep them warm so they would hatch. She left the nest only for short times, to hunt for food. During this period, her mate, the male robin, stayed nearby to guard her and the eggs.

Finally, four tiny, scrawny babies hatched out of the eggs. They were completely helpless. Their eyes were closed and they were too weak to move. They had no feathers, so their mother had to brood, or crouch over, them to keep them warm.

It was mostly the father robin's job to find food for the babies. All day long he searched for worms, beetles, grasshoppers, and other such creatures. When he found something, he flew back to the nest at once. He always landed on or near the nest, which made it jiggle. This movement of the nest told the babies that food had come.

At once, each baby stretched out its neck and opened its mouth as wide as it could! The father stuffed food into the mouth that seemed widest and hungriest. Then he flew off in search of another worm or insect.

In five days, the babies' eyes were open. They began to grow fluffy coats of feathers. Now they didn't need to be brooded as often, so the mother robin joined the father in hunting for food.

About two weeks after hatching, the young robins had all their feathers. But they didn't look a bit like their mother and father. Instead of having bright red breasts, the young robins' breasts were tan-colored and speckled with dark spots. As they grew older, their breasts would turn red.

By the time the youngsters began trying to fly, their mother left them. She went off to

build another nest, so as to rear another
family. The father stayed behind to look after
the young ones.

This was a dangerous time for the young
ones. A cat or other enemy might easily catch
them. But, before long, they became good
flyers, and were safe. Once they could fly, they
went off by themselves.

During the next few months, the mother
and father robins might have one or two more
families. All summer long, red-breasted adults
and speckle-breasted youngsters would be a
common sight running about on lawns.

But, by late autumn, the redbreasts would
be gone from the northern parts of the
country. They would move far enough south
to avoid the snow and bitter cold. Then, when
winter was over, they would return, to show
that spring had come again.

Chimney dwellers

Chimney Swifts are rather small birds, about only five inches (12.5 centimeters) long. They are well named, for they often rest and build their nests inside chimneys. And they certainly are swift, for they are among the fastest of all birds.

Except when sleeping or keeping eggs warm, Chimney Swifts spend almost all their time flying. They never perch in trees or run about on the ground. They get all their food while they fly—opening up their wide mouths to gulp down flying insects they meet in midair. They even build their nests as they fly, without once alighting.

To make a nest, the swifts break small dead twigs off trees. They fly at the twigs and snap them off by hitting them with their feet. Then they carry the twigs in their bills to a chimney, or perhaps a hollow tree. They glue the twigs to the inside wall of the chimney with their saliva, or spit, which is thick and sticky, like glue. They glue more twigs together to form a nest that looks like half a basket sticking out from the wall.

When a Chimney Swift rests inside a chimney, it can't sit as a robin does when perching on a branch. The swift digs its sharp toes into the side of the chimney. To keep from sliding down, it uses its tail as a prop.

At migration time, whole flocks of these

Flocks of Chimney Swifts often rest inside the tall chimneys of factories.

little birds will often rest inside a tall factory chimney. They fly around the chimney in a ring for a while. Then, some birds circle down into the chimney. More and more follow. The circle begins to look like a funnel-shaped cloud of smoke—but a cloud that's going down the chimney instead of rising up out of it!

54

European storks often make nests on the roofs of houses and factories. This stork's nest is on a church in Portugal.

A nest on a rooftop

In many parts of Europe, people invite a bird to make its nest on their roof! They'll even put a big basket, or a platform, on the roof, for the bird to build its nest on.

The bird is the big White Stork. People in The Netherlands, Germany, Poland, and other parts of Europe think that storks living on their roof will bring good luck. So, they make the birds welcome.

The storks spend the winter in South Africa. In the springtime, they fly back to

Europe. The male storks usually show up first. A male will pick out a good place for a nest, such as a chimney, a roof, a church tower, or even a telephone pole. There, he waits until a female stork comes to join him. Together, they build a nest.

A stork nest is a huge pile of sticks, earth, rags, grass, and paper, piled in layers. Often, a pair of storks will take over an old nest and build it up even higher. The storks collect their building material from the streets and fields. Sometimes, a stork will even steal a piece of clothing from a washline to use in building its nest!

When the female has laid all her eggs, she and the male take turns incubating them. The first babies hatch out after about thirty-two days. Both the mother and father bring them food, which at first is mostly worms. When the young birds are about seven weeks old, they begin to practice flying. They flap their wings and make little jumps. In a few more weeks, they can fly.

There is a legend that young storks feed and take care of their parents. But this isn't true. Young storks migrate to Africa in late summer, leaving their parents behind. The parents don't leave until early autumn.

Storks eat insects, fish, frogs, lizards, snakes, mice, rats, and other small creatures. They get their food by walking about in fields or wading in swamps, snapping up anything they find.

Stork Fables

At one time, children were often told that babies were brought by storks. That isn't true, of course.

There is an old fable that young storks take care of their elderly parents. But that's not true, either.

Apartment dwellers

The birds known as Purple Martins have been on friendly terms with people for a long time. They used to live in the villages of North American Indians. The Indians hung up hollow gourds with holes cut in them for doorways. The birds happily used these gourds for nests. The Indians liked having the Purple Martins around. The martins chased away crows and other birds that raided the Indians' crops.

Today, many people in North America put up birdhouses for Purple Martins to nest in. Martins like to live in large groups, or colonies. So, people buy, or make, very large birdhouses that have many rooms, each with its own doorway, for the martins to use. Such birdhouses become regular apartment houses for martin colonies.

A colony of martins does a lot of bustling and "arguing" before each pair of birds finally gets a nest going. First, early in spring, young males show up and battle each other for "rooms." When the females appear and pick

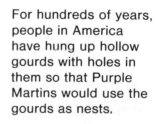

For hundreds of years, people in America have hung up hollow gourds with holes in them so that Purple Martins would use the gourds as nests.

Some people put up birdhouses that are like apartment houses for Purple Martins to nest in.

mates, there are more battles over the best places. Finally, older pairs of males and females arrive and simply take over the nicest "rooms"!

Once the "apartments" are all taken, the arguing stops. When the eggs begin to hatch in each nest, there's great excitement. The parents take turns feeding their young with flies, mosquitoes, and even wasps. The air around the nests seems filled with birds, coming and going and loudly whistling, chirping, and twittering.

By late August and early September, the young are full-grown fliers. The martins begin to leave their apartment house. Flocks of them come together, forming bigger and ever bigger flocks. Then they begin to fly south for the winter.

Noisy neighbors!

The Common Starling is a black bird speckled with purple and green and small white dots. A hundred years ago, there were no starlings in North America. But in 1890 and 1891, about eighty pairs from Europe were set free in New York City's Central Park. Today, the bird is a common sight strutting on lawns and roosting on buildings throughout America.

Starlings are noisy, pushy birds! They'll shove other birds aside to get food. They even steal food when they can. Suppose a starling and a robin are hunting on the same lawn. If the robin finds a worm, the starling may rush over and take the worm right out of the robin's bill! It's surprising, but the robin seldom puts up a fuss.

Starlings will also push other birds out of their nest and take it over for themselves. They like to nest in holes in tree trunks, or in small openings in the walls of houses and

A starling (left) will
sometimes steal a
worm right out of a
robin's bill!

buildings. They'll also happily nest in a
birdhouse, which they stuff with a padding of
sticks and straws or dried grass.

Hardly a city in North America or Europe
doesn't abound with these bold little birds.
They often roost by the dozen on window
ledges, trees, and even inside large, open
public buildings. Many people look upon them
as pests. They often chatter, squeak, and
whistle all night long, keeping people awake.
And they are rather messy.

In many places, people have tried to get rid
of starlings. But nothing has worked. The
starlings seem quite happy and able to live
alongside people—whether the people want
them or not!

City birds

Probably the best-known bird in North America, Europe, Australia, and New Zealand is the little House Sparrow. In America, this bird is often called an English Sparrow, because it was brought from England more than a hundred years ago.

While these birds aren't exactly tame, they do seem to want to live among people. They are seen all year long in cities, towns, and farm areas, even where winters are cold and

House Sparrows like to live near people, and can sometimes be tamed.

snowy. Sparrows can stay through the winter because there is plenty of food for them. In fact, they get much of their food from people.

Sparrows enjoy eating the bits of bread, rolls, and other baked foods that people often leave lying around. In spring, they'll gobble up seeds that people put in lawns, gardens, and farm fields. And in autumn, they eat ripe grain and grass seed.

House Sparrows also seem to prefer making their nests in things people have built. They'll nest on fire escapes, window ledges, traffic lights, and in rainspouts, as well as in cozy corners of buildings and houses. They often take over birdhouses that are put up for other birds, such as bluebirds. When they do nest in a tree, sparrows generally pick one that's close to a building.

The male sparrow picks the place for the nest, but both birds work on the nest. The nest is a large, bulky, untidy ball of grass, twigs, leaves, and perhaps a bit of string, lined with feathers. After the nest is finished, the female soon lays from three to seven eggs. These she incubates, or sits on, for about thirteen days.

When the babies hatch, the parents start hunting insects. At first, they eat any insect they catch. When they go back to the nest, they throw up what they have eaten and feed this to the babies. Later, the babies eat whole insects. Often, another adult sparrow will help

These two little House Sparrows are taking a bath in a garden pond.

the parents with the job of feeding their young. Sparrows can have three sets of babies during a summer, so they eat a lot of insects.

When the young birds first leave the nest, they stay close to their parents for a time, and beg food from them. But they soon learn to feed themselves. Then they join other young birds to form a large flock that stays together. The flock picks out a special tree, or other place, where all the sparrows roost at night. On summer evenings, you can often hear a flock of sparrows noisily twittering in their roosting place.

House Sparrows aren't as pretty as many other kinds of birds. They're sometimes dirty from the smoke and grime of the city. But a lot of people like them. And it's nice to be able to see and hear birds singing on a cold winter day in a snow-covered city!

To a Sparrow

by Francis Ledwige

There is no bird half so harmless,
None so sweetly rude as you,
None so common and so charmless,
None of virtues nude as you.

But for all your faults I love you,
For you linger with us still,
Though the wintry winds reprove you,
And the snow lies on the hill.

Skyscraper dwellers

Like House Sparrows, the birds we call city pigeons are true year-round city dwellers. In fact, they often live in the very busiest, noisiest parts of cities!

The city birds we call pigeons are really a kind of bird known as a Rock Dove. Wild Rock Doves usually live on cliffs by the sea and make their nests in caves.

Unlike sparrows, city pigeons are quite tame. They waddle about among crowds of people, looking for nuts, popcorn, or other goodies that have been dropped. They will walk right up to anyone who offers them a bit of bread or other food. Large flocks of pigeons gather in city parks, where people often go to feed them.

The pigeons carry on their lives in the middle of all the city's noise, smoke, and bustle. They build their nests on the ledges of tall skyscrapers and on the girders of bridges. The nest is a loose platform of stiff twigs. While the female stays at the nesting place, the male goes out to search for twigs. He tests each twig for proper stiffness by shaking it in his bill. He brings the twigs back, one at a time, to his mate.

When baby pigeons hatch, their eyes are closed and they are helpless. But the parents don't have to go out right away to hunt food for them as most birds must do for their

City pigeons are good at finding food wherever they can. These pigeons are picking up grain spilled from the horse's "lunch."

babies. Both a mother and father pigeon are able to make a milky, fatty sort of liquid inside their throat. They feed this liquid, called pigeon's milk, to the babies by squirting it into their mouths.

As the babies, which are known as squabs (skwahbz), grow older, their parents bring them fruit, caterpillars, and other things to eat. After four or five weeks, the young ones are out on their own—waddling about among the crowds of people.

Pigeons of the city seem like friendly, likable birds. Unfortunately, however, they sometimes are disease carriers. Many people regard them as serious pests.

Other birds of Town and City

European Robin

(Europe)
The European Robin, or "redbreast," is only about half as big as the American Robin. It has red on its head and on its breast.

Blue Jay

(North America)

Willie Wagtail
(Australia)

Cardinal
(North America)

Birds of Farmland and Open Country

A trickster

It was springtime. A large black and white cat trotted across the farm field. Suddenly, she stopped in the middle of a step, as cats do, with one paw off the ground. She had seen something.

A bird lay on the ground ahead of her. It was a fairly large bird, about ten inches (25 centimeters) long, with brownish back and wings and a white breast. It seemed sick, or hurt. It was panting and gasping, feebly.

The cat became interested. She took a few cautious steps toward the bird. At once, the bird gave a shrill shriek and began to flutter away. It dragged one wing on the ground, as if it might be broken. It shrieked again. The cat stopped and stared. The bird also stopped, and lay panting and shrieking.

The cat flattened herself against the ground and began to creep forward. The bird fluttered away, helplessly, giving screams of fear.

photographs on pages 68–69

Crowned Cranes on an African plain, and a killdeer

Another bird now appeared overhead, shrieking loudly. It was the other's mate. Apparently, it was trying to help the injured bird by getting the cat's attention so that the other bird could escape.

But the cat paid no attention. She sensed an easy victory and speeded up her movement toward the prey. The injured bird managed to keep fluttering and flopping away from her. But, surely, the cat would catch up to the poor creature before long!

Farther and farther across the field they went, the cat pursuing the frightened, fluttering bird. But, suddenly, the bird stopped shrieking. Calmly, it spread its wings, flew up into the air, and headed back across the field!

The cat stared after it for a moment. Then she sat down and began to lick her paw. She seemed to be trying to show that she didn't care if the bird had escaped—and didn't care if she had been fooled into believing it was hurt and helpless!

The bird skimmed over the field and came down just about where the cat had first seen it. Four baby birds hurried to it. It was their mother. The cat would have discovered these babies. But by acting as if she had a broken wing, the mother had tricked the cat into following her far away. This is how these birds, which are called killdeers, protect their eggs and babies.

Killdeers got their name because of the sound they often make—*kil-deee, kil-deee.* They belong to a family of birds that mostly live along shores. But killdeers like to live in open meadows and fields. They especially like plowed farm fields, where there are plenty of insects. They're good friends to farmers, because they eat lots of the kinds of insects that damage farm crops.

Killdeers live mostly in North and South America, but sometimes wander accidentally to Ireland, England, and Scotland. They are not the only kind of birds that protect their babies by pretending to be hurt. Many kinds of birds that make their nests on the ground also play this "trick."

The biggest birds

The world's three biggest birds live on huge, flat, open plains in Africa, Australia, and South America. These birds look much alike and live in much the same way. None of them can fly. They walk and run about on their two sturdy legs.

The biggest of *all* birds is the ostrich of Africa. A male ostrich may be as much as eight feet (2.4 meters) tall. It may weigh as much as 330 pounds (150 kilograms).

However, this big, heavy bird runs very fast. An ostrich can run forty miles (64 kilometers)

Ostriches live in flocks in dry parts of Africa. They are the biggest of all birds.

an hour. That's almost as fast as a race horse can run. Baby ostriches can run almost as soon as they hatch. When they are only a month old, they can run nearly as fast as a grown-up ostrich.

There's a good reason for this. There are lions and other dangerous animals where ostriches live. But ostriches cannot fly to get away from danger, so they have to be able to run away.

It isn't true that an ostrich will try to hide by burying its head in the sand. However, an ostrich will often squat down and stretch its neck along the ground. Without its long neck sticking up, it is hard to see from a distance.

Ostriches generally live together in large flocks. Sometimes these flocks number up to six hundred birds. The birds roam about in search of food, which is mostly plants. Because they live on dry plains and deserts, they often have to search for water. But they can go for a long time without drinking, if they have enough green plants to eat.

A father ostrich is a good father and does a lot of the work of caring for the babies. He makes the nest by scooping out a shallow pit in the sand. He then sits down in it. The mother ostrich lays her eggs in front of him and he pushes them under himself. He then incubates the eggs each day from late afternoon until early the next morning. The mother incubates them the rest of the time.

Emus gathered at a water hole in New South Wales, Australia.

When the babies hatch, both the father and mother look after them. In time of danger, both parents protect the babies. If a dangerous animal appears, one parent may attack it, while the other leads the babies to safety. An ostrich can fight very well if it has to. A kick from one of its big, two-toed feet can rip open a lion's body!

The bird called an emu (EE myoo) lives mostly on dry plains and deserts in Australia. It is the next largest bird after the ostrich—about five or six feet (1.5 to 1.8 m) tall. It weighs about one hundred pounds (45 kg). Like ostriches, emus are fast runners. They live in small flocks and eat leaves, grass, fruit, and insects.

The rhea (REE uh) lives on grassy plains in South America. Rheas are about five feet (1.5 m) tall, and weigh about fifty pounds (22.5 kg). They, too, are fast, fast runners. They usually live in small flocks of twenty or thirty. Rheas eat mostly leaves and grass, and some insects and small animals.

Father rheas and emus do all the work of taking care of their babies. They make the nests and incubate the eggs. When the babies hatch, the fathers stay with them until they can take care of themselves.

male Rhea

A long-legged hunter

The Secretary Bird of Africa hunts lizards, snakes, and other small animals by stamping about in the grass.

Stalking through the clumps of yellow-green grass that dotted the sandy African plain came a very tall bird. It marched along with great dignity on two long, slim legs. As it walked, it peered at the ground. From time to time it stamped one foot, noisily.

There was a reason for the foot stamping. Millions of small creatures lurked in the grass of the great plain—grasshoppers, lizards, mouselike animals, and others. The stamp of the bird's foot might startle one of them into darting out of its hiding place. Then, with a quick jab of its beak, the bird could pick up an easy meal.

However, the bird's stamping suddenly startled a much larger creature. It was a cobra—a deadly, poisonous snake! With an enraged hiss, it reared up to challenge the bird! But the bird neither ran nor flew away. It spread its wings and stalked fearlessly toward the snake.

The snake struck! Its head shot forward to give the bird a poisonous bite on its leg. But the bird simply flicked one wing in front of itself, like a shield. Then it lashed out with its foot. In one swift, hard kick, it smashed the cobra's body, killing it. Bending down, the

bird picked up the snake in its bill, and swallowed it!

This long-legged African bird is known as the Secretary Bird. While Secretary Birds eat mostly lizards, insects, and other small creatures, they'll gladly feast on snakes, even those that are as much as six feet (1.8 meters) long! They kill snakes by stomping on them or kicking them. Poisonous snakes can't hurt the birds because they can't bite through the birds' tough, scale-covered legs or do harm to their wing feathers.

Secretary Birds can fly, but they seldom do. They spend most of their time walking over the grassy plains. A Secretary Bird can actually walk faster than a human can run. And the birds can run *very* fast.

A secretary is a person whose work is to write letters and keep records of things. Why are these birds named after such a person?

The birds were given their name in the 1700's, when one of them was first brought to England. At that time, most secretaries were men, and most men wore wigs. Secretaries did their writing with quill pens, which were made from feathers. When not using their pens, they often stuck them into the back of their wigs. The African bird has a cluster of feathers sticking out of the back of its head—and this made people think of a secretary, with several pens stuck in his wig. So, the bird was called a Secretary Bird.

Burrowing Owl

A Burrowing Owl uses the old burrow of a fox, badger, or other animal for its home.

A borrowed burrow

The sun is setting on a prairie in North America. On a little hump of earth, in front of a hole, stands a small, long-legged owl. Slowly, it turns its head almost all the way around in a circle. Its wide eyes peer carefully over the prairie.

In the distance, a coyote trots along, heading straight toward the owl. The owl makes a sort of bowing motion several times. Then it pops into the hole and vanishes from sight. The coyote trots on.

This kind of owl is known as a Burrowing Owl. Its home and hiding place is an underground tunnel. Usually, a Burrowing Owl takes over an empty burrow some animal has made—a fox den, a badger hole, or a prairie dog burrow. If it can't find such a place, it digs its own, with its feet.

Like all other kinds of owls, Burrowing Owls are meat-eaters. They hunt at night, and sometimes in the daylight. Flying fairly close to the ground, they rise to snatch insects out of the air, and dive to snatch small creatures on the ground. They'll eat beetles, lizards, grasshoppers, ground squirrels, snakes, and small birds.

At mating time, a pair of Burrowing Owls will share the same burrow. They also like to be close to the burrows of other owls. The female owl lays her eggs far down at the end of the tunnel. When the babies hatch, both the mother and father owls hunt food for the little owlets.

baby Burrowing Owls

Birds that ride on animals!

A great many kinds of animals live on the vast plains of Africa. And many of those animals become "mobile homes" for birds known as oxpeckers! An antelope, a long-necked giraffe, or a huge rhinoceros often has two or three oxpeckers living on its back for days at a time.

Oxpeckers don't ride about on an animal just for fun. They do it because that's how they get their food. The birds walk over the animal, searching for ticks and other insects, many of which burrow down into an animal's skin. The oxpeckers gladly gobble up these creatures.

You might think that it would annoy an animal to have birds walking on it and pecking it with their sharp bills. But, actually, it is a real relief for the animals to have the birds get rid of the insects, which bother them. The animals seem to know what the birds are doing, and are glad to have them do it.

Oxpeckers don't stay only with wild animals. They also live on tame cattle that belong to farmers' herds. At night, the birds may leave the animal and fly up into a nearby tree to roost. But, usually, they'll stay with the animal, even when it lies down to sleep. By staying with it, they won't have to search for a new "home" in the morning!

Oxpecker on a rhinoceros

The African bird called an Oxpecker spends most of its time on the back of a rhinoceros or other large animal. It feeds on insects that have burrowed into the animal's skin.

The prairie hawk

A large bird circled low over a farm field in western North America. It was all white except for its legs and the back of its wings, which were reddish-brown. It was a Ferruginous (fuh ROO juh nuhs) Hawk. These hawks are named for the color of their legs and wings. The word *ferruginous* means "reddish-brown" or "rust-colored."

The field had just been harvested. The green plants were all gone. Only the dark dirt remained. The hawk seemed to be studying the field.

In a few moments, the bird saw what it was looking for. Some of the dirt had been pushed up into little piles by gophers (GOH fuhrz), small ratlike animals that live in underground tunnels.

The hawk glided down. Softly as a feather falling into snow, it landed by one of the piles. For a time, it waited. Then, there was a stirring in the earth. A new pile of dirt started to form. A gopher was working just beneath the surface.

In an instant, the hawk opened its wings and rose a short way into the air. Then it dropped. Its feet stabbed into the pile of dirt. A moment later it flapped up into the air, the body of the gopher dangling from its claws. The gopher never knew what hit it. It was killed instantly by the hawk's grip.

Ferruginous Hawks are about two feet (60 centimeters) long. They are birds of the prairies and farmlands. They are a help to farmers, as they eat mainly gophers, ground squirrels, and prairie dogs—all animals that damage crops.

Apartment builders

On the plains of southern Africa there are flocks of birds that work together to put up "apartment buildings" in which they all live! They are the kind of birds known as Social Weavers—social because they like to live together and weavers because they weave their nests out of grass and straw.

Social Weavers are small, sparrow-sized birds. They live in flocks of several hundred. They begin their nest-building in the middle of summer—which in southern Africa is around Christmastime. The birds build their nest in a tree that's all by itself, with no other trees close by. Or, they may put the nest on the crosspiece of a telegraph pole.

The weavers work in pairs—males and females that are mates. They search the nearby plain for dry grass stalks and straw, which they bring back to the tree or pole. They weave this together to form a huge dome, as much as ten feet (3 meters) high and fifteen feet (4.5 m) wide. It looks like a big, shaggy haystack. But it is so tightly woven that it is waterproof. Rain can't soak through it.

The dome is actually just the nest's roof. When it's finished, each pair of birds goes to work to make an "apartment." This is a small, roundish room under the dome. It has a short tunnel that hangs down to the underside of

Social Weaver

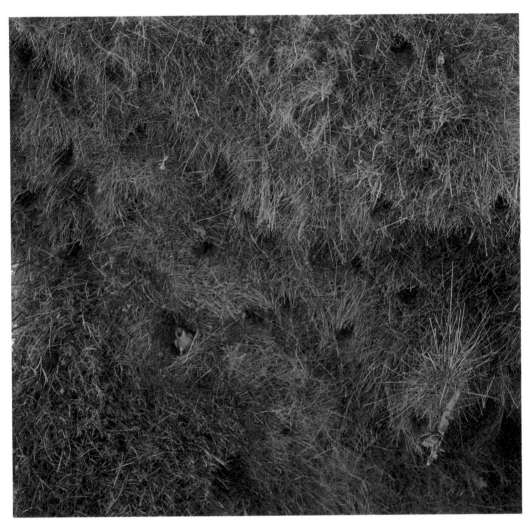

A Social Weaver nest looks like a big, shaggy haystack. It has several hundred "rooms" in which the birds lay their eggs and raise their young.

the nest. There may be as many as three hundred rooms in a very large Social Weaver nest!

The female lays her eggs in the room she and her mate built. The babies are hatched and reared in the rooms. Even after the young ones are grown, the birds stay in the nest most of the year. They even mend it if it gets damaged.

Bird "criminals"

Spring has come to the English countryside. In the tall grass and bushes of a field, many bird nests are hidden. In most of these, the female birds are sitting, getting ready to lay their eggs.

A gray-bodied bird with a gray and white striped breast moves about in the field. It seems to be looking for something. From time to time, one of the female birds sitting in a nest notices it. She sets up an excited twittering. Often, her mate, perched nearby, joins in. All these birds somehow know that this gray stranger is up to no good!

The gray bird is a female cuckoo—a "criminal" in the bird world! She is looking for a place to lay an egg. She will lay it in the nest of another bird. Usually, the result will be the destruction of the other bird's eggs and family! Somehow, other birds sense that a cuckoo is a danger to them.

The cuckoo is looking for a special nest. She wants the nest of the bird called a Lesser Whitethroat. After a time, she finds one—a loose bowl of grass and twigs among the low branches of a bush. The female whitethroat is on the nest. She has laid one egg, and will lay more in days to come.

The female cuckoo lurks nearby, waiting her chance. It comes in the afternoon, when the whitethroat leaves for a few moments to get food or water. At once, the cuckoo flies straight to the nest. In an instant, she has laid an egg. Then she picks up the whitethroat egg in her bill and flies away. The egg the cuckoo has laid looks almost exactly like the egg she has taken away.

Cuckoos lay their eggs in the nests of other birds. After laying her own egg, a cuckoo will steal one of the other birds' eggs.

The whitethroat soon returns. She squats down on the egg, accepting it as her own. A dozen days pass. The whitethroat has laid the rest of her eggs. They are not yet due to hatch for a good many days. Now, however, the cuckoo egg begins to hatch. After a time, it cracks open and the baby cuckoo pushes its way out.

The newly hatched bird has no feathers, and its eyes are closed. It seems weak and completely helpless. It lies in the nest without moving and without making a sound.

About ten hours later, the baby cuckoo begins to move. The mother whitethroat has left the nest, and the cuckoo is alone with the whitethroat eggs. It begins to wiggle around the bottom of the nest. When it comes to an egg, it burrows down beneath it. Then, with the egg on its back, it pushes upward—and upward. Finally, it manages to push the egg out of the nest!

The baby cuckoo does this with every other whitethroat egg. If there had been any whitethroat babies in the nest, it would have done the same to them. The eggs it pushes out of the nest fall to the ground. Some are smashed, others simply lie there and never hatch. No baby whitethroats will ever come out of them.

The baby cuckoo has a sort of "message," or instinct, in its body that makes it wiggle about for a while and push up at anything it bumps into. This is an instinct that helps it survive. By getting rid of the whitethroat babies, the young cuckoo has made sure it will not have to share food with them.

The mother whitethroat returns to the nest. Does she see that her eggs are gone? Does she realize what has happened? No, she does not. All she knows is that there is a baby bird in the nest and it is begging for food. Her

A baby cuckoo pushes all other eggs, and even baby birds, out of its nest.

**warbler feeding
a young cuckoo**

A young cuckoo is often much bigger than the adult birds that take care of it.

instincts tell her to feed it. From now on, she devotes herself to hunting for food and bringing it to the baby cuckoo, which gets bigger and fatter each day!

Every year, in many parts of the world, a great many birds become foster parents to a baby cuckoo. Cuckoos never build a nest, and they never rear their own young. They always get another bird to do it for them. The bird's own eggs or babies are almost always destroyed by the baby cuckoo.

Cuckoos don't all choose the same kind of bird as a foster parent. The bird that a female cuckoo chooses to give her egg to is usually the same kind of bird that reared her when she was hatched. Often, this will be a much smaller bird than a cuckoo—so that the baby cuckoo towers like a giant over its foster parent!

Are cuckoos truly "criminals"? No, of course not. They are simply doing what their instincts *make* them do. This is how cuckoos are "designed" to live and survive.

The cuckoo is a giddy bird,
　　No other is as she,
That flits across the meadow,
　　That sings in every tree.
A nest she never buildeth,
　　A vagrant she doth roam;
Her music is but tearful—
Cuckoo—cuckoo—cuckoo!
　　"I nowhere have a home."

　　　　from *The Cuckoo*
　　　　Author Unknown

Parakeets

The sprightly little birds that many people
call parakeets, and keep as pets, are actually
Budgerigars (BUHJ uhr ee gahrz), or budgies.
Their home is in Australia. There they live in
large, noisy flocks on vast grassy plains dotted
here and there with trees. They eat mostly
grass seed. When the seed in one place is
eaten up, the flock flies to a new place. Thus,
budgerigars are often on the move.

But life is not always easy on the grassland.
Sometimes, no rain falls for many months and
waterholes dry up. The flocks must then fly in
search of water. If none is found soon enough,
hundreds of thousands of the little birds might
perish.

However, budgies are fitted for such a life. They are able to go for months without drinking, as long as they have enough ripe grass seed to eat. And after each rain, the birds can breed, laying many thousands of eggs, and making up for the loss of any birds that died.

After a rainfall, flocks of budgies gather in the branches of mallee scrub trees. There are so many green birds on each branch, the tree looks as if it had burst into blossom with greenery. Pairs of birds crawl about the branches looking for cracks. Using their bills, they chip away at these cracks to make them bigger. The holes they make then become nests in which the females lay their eggs.

The word *budgerigar* comes from the language of the Aborigines, the first people who lived in Australia. Long ago, the Aborigines hunted the little birds because they were good eating.

The butcherbird

The gray and black bird sat on a barbed-wire fence running along a road near a farm in the southern United States. It was motionless as a rock—but all the time it carefully watched the ground.

Suddenly, the bird darted from its perch. It had spied a small brown form scampering through the grass—a field mouse. The bird stabbed with its beak, but the mouse dodged and turned to fight! It leaped at the bird. However, the bird stood its ground and stabbed again. After a moment, the mouse lost its courage. It turned to flee.

But it was doomed. The bird darted after it. With its sharply hooked beak, the bird seized the mouse by the neck. Fiercely, it twisted and shook the mouse, biting into the furry creature. The mouse was soon dead.

Picking up the mouse in its feet, the bird flew back to the fence. It pushed the mouse's body onto one of the sharp barbs that stuck out along all the fence wires. Once the mouse was firmly hung up on the barb, the bird began to eat it.

This fierce bird, smaller than an American Robin, was a Loggerhead Shrike (shryk). Like all shrikes, it has another name. If you have ever been in a butcher shop, you've seen that butchers hang large pieces of meat on hooks in special cold rooms. So, because of the way shrikes hang up the "meat" they catch, they are often called "butcherbirds."

There are many different kinds of shrikes living in all parts of the world. They all hunt such creatures as mice, grasshoppers, beetles, small birds, lizards, and even bats and snakes. Any creature they catch is usually hung up on a thorn, a sharp, broken branch, or a wire. They sometimes kill more than they can eat. Sometimes, when live prey is scarce, they will return and eat what they have hung up.

The Loggerhead Shrike, or butcher bird, hangs its prey on a barbed wire fence, on a sharp branch, or on a thorn.

Other birds of farmland and open country

Great Bustard

(Europe, Asia)

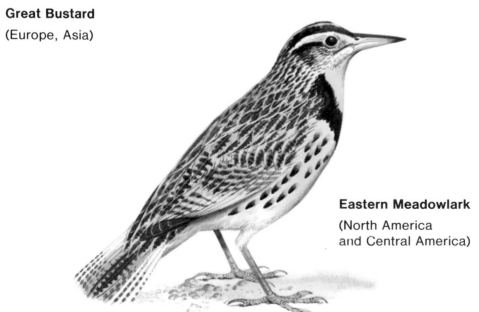

Eastern Meadowlark

(North America
and Central America)

Magpie
(Europe, Africa,
Asia, North America)

Hoopoe
(Europe, Africa, Asia)

Marabou Stork
(Africa)

Birds of Woodlands and Forests

Life in the woods

It is a chilly March morning in a woods in North America. The sun is just about to rise. On a huge old log stands a bird with handsomely decorated feathers—a male Ruffed Grouse.

The grouse has claimed as its "territory" the small patch of woods in which the old log lies. If another male should come into this territory, the grouse will fight it! The two birds will peck and kick and beat each other with their wings. Finally, one bird will give up and run away. The winner will keep the territory.

photographs on pages 102–103

a female pheasant in a forest clearing, and a Ruffed Grouse

To the grouse, the old log is the most important part of the territory. The bird comes to the log each sunrise and sunset to do a special task.

He leans back, pressing his tail against the log. He spreads his wings, like a person stretching. Then he begins to beat the air with his wings, moving them back and forth slowly at first, then speeding up until they move so fast they become a blur. A sound like a rumble of distant thunder fills the air.

About every five minutes, all during sunrise, the grouse beats his wings this way for about ten seconds. The booming sound carries far through the woods. The bird makes this noise for the same reason a robin sings its spring song—to call a female to come be his mate, and to warn other males to stay out of his territory.

As the gray light of dawn begins to fill the woods, a female grouse hears the booming. At once, she flies straight toward the sound.

The female alights near the log. The male peers at her suspiciously. He hops off the log and walks stiffly toward her. He wiggles his head and hisses. If this newcomer wants a fight, he'll give it one! But the female pays no attention to him. She begins to peck at a tender young dandelion plant. The male realizes she isn't an "invader." He grows calmer. In time, they will mate.

After mating, the female grouse searches

until she finds a clearing—a broad place in the woods where no trees are standing. She finds a pile of leaves close beside an old stump. She pushes her body into the leaves to make a shallow, scooped-out place. She settles into it. Each day, for fifteen days, she lays a small pale-brown egg.

For the next twenty-four days, the female lies huddled over the eggs. She leaves the nest only once or twice a day to get food and

water. When she comes back, she turns each egg over to make sure that all parts of the egg will get enough warmth.

While the female incubates her eggs, both she and they are in constant danger. Foxes, raccoons, opossums, skunks, and many other animals that prowl the woods will gladly eat both her and her eggs. Hawks and owls are also her deadly enemies. However, as she lies on the leaves, her body blends into them so well it's almost impossible to see her. Once, a fox trots by and never even notices her.

On the twenty-fourth day, the female hears noises and feels movement in the eggs beneath her. She begins to walk nervously around the

nest as the babies start to peck their way out of their shells. A few hours later, they are all out. At first, the baby grouse are wet and scrawny-looking, with closed eyes. But, quite soon, they are dry and fluffy, with wide, bright eyes.

The odor of the empty eggshells would soon attract the attention of many animals. The mother grouse somehow "knows" she must get the young ones away from the nest. She leads them off into the clearing. They quickly learn to peck up every small, moving insect they see. They follow their mother about all day. At night, they all sleep huddled under her wings.

The days pass. The chicks learn to hide when their mother gives the *preent-preent* sound that means "danger." They dart for the closest cover and crouch without moving. When they hear their mother make a *peeeer* sound, they scurry out of hiding and join her.

As the young ones grow older, they learn to eat many kinds of plants, and stop eating insects. They now sleep in a circle around their mother, instead of under her wings. After about two weeks, they can fly well enough to reach the low branches of trees. Then, they and their mother sleep in a tree each night.

By autumn, the young grouse are just about full grown. There are fewer of them now, for some have been killed and eaten by other creatures of the woods.

The bodies of all the grouse in the woods now begin to change. The birds store up fat from gorging on wild grapes, apples, acorns, and nuts. Their bodies and legs begin to grow a warm, downy covering. Their toes sprout little thorny hooks. These will act as snowshoes to keep the birds from sinking into the snow that will cover the ground through the heart of winter.

Some of these young birds will be "boomers" next spring, beating their wings while standing on an old log. Others will become mothers with families of their own to care for through the spring and summer.

A bill for worms

On a moonlit night, in a swampy forest, a large bird with a long bill walks slowly over a patch of muddy ground.

    The bird walks with its head close to the ground. It pauses. Then it pushes its bill down into the soft, damp earth. In the earth, a worm is crawling. The tip of the bird's bill touches it. In an instant, the worm is swallowed up!

woodcock

The colors of a woodcock's feathers help the bird blend into its surroundings.

The long, thin bill of the bird called a woodcock is a marvelous tool for getting the bird's favorite food, earthworms. The woodcock can poke its long bill into soft earth, down to where worms are plentiful. The tip of the bill can be wiggled, like a finger. The woodcock uses it to feel for worms. Even though the bill is deep in the ground, the bird is able to open it and swallow the worm.

Woodcocks do their hunting where the ground is soft. So, they live mostly in swampy, wet woods, where the ground is moist and muddy. They hunt at night, because that's when earthworms are most active, crawling about near the surface.

During the day, the birds stay hidden in dark places under trees or bushes. Their feathers, which are the color of dead leaves, help them blend into their surroundings, so that they're almost invisible. And their huge eyes are set so far back, they can see in all directions without turning their head.

Woodcocks are good flyers. But they spend a lot of time on the ground, and even make their nests on the ground. A woodcock's nest is just a shallow hollow, scooped out of the ground and lined with a few leaves. If a mother woodcock feels her babies are in danger, she'll sometimes move them out of the nest. She takes them between her feet, one at a time, and flies with them to a safer place.

The kiwi of New Zealand

One of the strangest of all birds dwells in
some of the moist forests of New Zealand. It
has feathery "whiskers" around its bill, its
body feathers resemble a shaggy coat of hair,
and it has no tail feathers. Its wings are so
tiny they can't even be seen, and, of course, it
cannot fly. It is called a kiwi (KEE wee),
probably because of the sound the male
makes.

In some ways, a kiwi is a lot like another
kind of bird that lives in damp woods, the
woodcock. Like a woodcock, the kiwi has a

long, slim, bendable bill that it pokes into soft earth in search of worms. And, like a woodcock, a kiwi hides by day, and hunts mostly by night.

A kiwi is about eighteen to twenty-two inches (45 to 50 centimeters) long. For its size, a female kiwi lays a *very* large egg. In fact, a four-pound (1.8-kilogram) kiwi lays an egg weighing one pound (0.45 kg)—one-fourth of her own weight!

At egg-laying time, pairs of male and female kiwis dig winding underground tunnels among roots of trees or under logs or rocks. The mother kiwi lays her egg in the tunnel. However, it is the male who incubates it. And when the young kiwi is ready to leave the nest, it is the father who takes it out into the world.

A holiday bird

Why is the turkey, which comes from North America, named after a country in the Middle East? It's because of a mistake.

The Spanish found the American bird in Mexico and brought it to Europe more than four hundred years ago. The English thought it was like a bird they called a turkey, and gave it the same name. This other bird was actually from Africa, but may have come to England by way of Turkish lands—thus the name. After it was known that the two birds were different, the name turkey was mistakenly kept for the American bird.

Most turkeys that people eat on holidays are raised on farms. But there are many wild turkeys living in woods in parts of North America. These wild turkeys only weigh about half as much as the domestic, or tame, turkeys. By day, they walk about in search of food—mostly seeds and nuts, but also grasshoppers, beetles, wild grapes, and berries. In the evening, they fly up into low branches of trees to spend the night.

At mating time, in the spring, each male turkey tries to attract as many females as he can. He does this by puffing himself up, spreading his feathers, and strutting about. He grunts, makes his *gobble-gobble* sound, and shakes his feathers. A male may soon "collect" several females.

Benjamin Franklin, the American statesman, wanted to make the wild turkey, not the Bald Eagle, the national bird of the United States.

wild turkeys
The male turkey (right) has puffed himself up and spread his tail to attract the female.

After a female turkey mates, she hurries off into the woods to make a nest. She scoops out a hollow under a bush and lays as many as twenty eggs. She incubates the eggs for about twenty-eight days. When she has to leave them to get food for herself, she covers the eggs with leaves and grass to hide them.

When the baby turkeys hatch, they are able to walk about and look for food right away. Their mother shows them how to search and scratch the ground to find food. During winter, the females and their young form a large flock and stay together. The male turkeys form a separate flock.

Owls of the woods

Creatures that live in fields and meadows, under open skies, fear the hawk and the falcon. But for creatures of the woods, the most feared enemy is the owl. A number of kinds of owls live in forests throughout the world. All are fierce, skillful hunters.

An owl of the woods, such as a North American Barred Owl, usually hunts at night. It has sharp eyes that can see well in just the

Barred Owl

faintest bit of light. It has such keen ears it can hear the faintest of sounds. It can hear the tiny sounds of a mouse's feet from fifty yards (45 meters) away. The owl turns its head until it locates the exact place from which the sounds come. Then it flies straight toward that place.

If the owl were any other kind of bird, the sounds of its wings might drown out the sounds of the mouse. But because of special wing feathers, an owl makes hardly any noise when it flies. It can hear the mouse clearly—but the mouse can't hear the owl.

If there is even the faintest gleam of moonlight, the owl will see the mouse at a distance of about six feet (1.8 m). But even if the night is pitch black, it doesn't matter. The owl can tell exactly where the mouse is from the noise it makes. Even though it can't see the mouse, the owl reaches out and grabs it with both feet, killing it instantly.

Most wood owls are large birds, from more than a foot (30 centimeters) to two feet (60 cm) long. Depending on their size, they hunt mice, rats, squirrels, rabbits, birds, frogs, worms, and insects. The Great Horned Owl, which lives in places other than woods, also preys on woodchucks, skunks, and even cats. It is a fierce hunter, known as "the tiger of the air"!

Wood owls make their nest and lay their eggs in holes in tree trunks, in hollow stumps,

Great Horned Owl

or in old, empty nests of other large birds. Owls feed their babies the same things they eat.

Although wood owls are night creatures, they can see in daylight. An owl is often "up and around" in the daytime, and this may get it into trouble. Other birds of the woods hate and fear owls. A Blue Jay, seeing an owl, will set up a tremendous chattering, to warn all other creatures that danger is near. And flocks of crows will actually attack any owl they see, and attempt to drive it away.

Gray Owl and crows
Flocks of crows will try to drive away any owl they see during the day.

The Owl

by Barry Cornwall

In the hollow tree, in the old gray tower,
  The spectral owl doth dwell;
Dull, hated, despised, in the sunshine hour,
  But at dusk he's abroad and well!
Not a bird of the forest e'er mates with him;
  All mock him outright by day;
But at night, when the woods grow still and dim,
  The boldest will shrink away!
    O, when the night falls, and roosts the fowl,
    Then, then, is the reign of the hornèd owl!

And the owl hath a bride, who is fond and bold,
  And loveth the wood's deep gloom;
And, with eyes like the shine of the moonstone cold,
  She awaiteth her ghastly groom;
Not a feather she moves, not a carol she sings,
  As she waits in her tree so still;
But when her heart heareth his flapping wings,
  She hoots out her welcome shrill!
    O, when the moon shines, and dogs do howl,
    Then, then, is the joy of the hornèd owl!

Mourn not for the owl, nor his gloomy plight!
   The owl hath his share of good:
If a prisoner he be in the broad daylight,
   He is lord in the dark greenwood!
Nor lonely the bird, nor his ghastly mate,
   They are unto each other a pride;
Thrice fonder, perhaps, since a strange, dark fate
   Hath rent them from all beside!
     So, when the night falls, the dogs do howl,
     Sing ho! for the reign of the hornèd owl!
       We know not alway
       Who are kings by day,
     But the king of the night is the bold brown owl!

The mound builders

In parts of Australia there is a kind of woods
known as mallee scrub. In these woods live
chicken-sized birds called Mallee Fowl. These
birds spend most of each year building and
looking after "incubators" in which they keep
their eggs!

Mallee Fowl

Mallee Fowl of Australia build a big mound in which to lay their eggs.

Each year, in autumn, a male Mallee Fowl, sometimes with help from his mate, begins to dig a pit. Scraping and scratching with his feet, he digs a pit about three feet (0.9 meter) deep and nine feet (2.7 m) wide. He fills this pit with a big pile of dead leaves, twigs, and tree bark. Then he covers the pile with a thick layer of sand, forming a mound four or five feet (1.2 to 1.5 m) high. All this work takes several months.

During the next few months, the male will open up the mound every five or ten days so that his mate can lay an egg in it. Each time, he covers up the mound again, so the egg is buried deep inside.

The heat inside the mound, and from the sun baking down, incubates the eggs. For the next seven months, the male visits the mound each day to check its temperature. If it seems to him that the eggs need more heat, he covers the mound with more sand. If it seems the eggs are getting too much heat, he opens up the mound for a time so it can cool.

Finally, one at a time, the eggs hatch. The babies must dig and push their way through a yard (0.9 m) or more of sand. Sometimes this takes a baby bird as long as fifteen hours!

When a baby finally breaks through the sand, its parents are usually nowhere near. Even if they were, they would pay no attention. For all the care they give to incubating their eggs, they give none at all to their babies!

However, a baby Mallee Fowl is well able to look after itself. It can run soon after it comes out of its mound. It knows how to scratch the ground for seeds and insects to eat. And, within twenty-four hours it is able to fly up into the low branches of a tree to spend the night.

The red-headed forester

From time to time in many a woods in North America there's a sound like someone thumping rapidly on a drum. This sound is made by one of the most important "citizens" in the woods—a Pileated Woodpecker. *Pileated* (PY lee ay tihd) means "having a pointed cluster of feathers on the head." A Pileated Woodpecker has such feathers on its head. They look like a pointed red cap.

Pileated Woodpeckers

The woodpecker makes its drumming sound
by hammering its bill on a tree limb or trunk.
During fall and winter, a male Pileated
Woodpecker often does this hammering to
make it known that he's in his territory. In
spring, he hammers to attract a mate and to
tell other males that this is his territory. The
sound carries far through the woods. If a
female woodpecker hears the sound, she will
fly straight to it.

But a lot of a Pileated Woodpecker's
hammering is done simply to get food. Many
of the trees in a woods are filled with insects.
Ants called carpenter ants make nests in tree
trunks, usually dead ones. Some kinds of
beetles live in tree trunks until they become
adults. These ants and beetles are a Pileated
Woodpecker's main food.

Somehow, a Pileated Woodpecker seems to
know exactly which trees have insects in
them. To get at the creatures, the bird chisels
holes with its sharp bill. When it uncovers an
insect, it pokes out a long, sticky, spiky
tongue. The insect gets caught on the tongue
and is pulled into the woodpecker's mouth.

A Pileated Woodpecker chisels holes in
trees by rapidly punching its bill into the
wood. This gouges out big chips of wood. It
seems a wonder that the bird doesn't hurt its
bill or jar its brain—but, of course, nature has
seen to it that this can't happen. The
woodpecker's bill is a tough, sturdy chisel, as

A Pileated Woodpecker bores holes in trees to find insects. It scoops out the insects with its long, spiky tongue.

good and as strong as any wood chisel made by humans. And the bird's brain is protected by skull bones that are almost as hard as concrete!

Pileated Woodpeckers also chisel holes in tree trunks to make nests. Inside the hole, the mother woodpecker lays her eggs on a pile of leftover wood chips.

Red Crossbill

A crossbill's bill is a special
tool for opening pine cones.

Pine tree dweller

Forests of spruce, fir, and pine trees are home for a little bird with one of the oddest of all bills. This bird's bill looks as if it is shaped all wrong. The top part of the bill curves down and the bottom part curves up. Thus, the two parts cross one another. Because of this strange bill, these birds are called crossbills.

It might seem that a crossbill would have a problem getting anything to eat. But, actually, the crossbill's bill is exactly what the bird needs to get its kind of food.

The crossbill eats the seeds of such trees as the pine, spruce, and fir—which is why it lives where those trees are plentiful. However, the seeds are inside pine cones. The crossbill has to get the seeds out of the cones, and that's what its bill is for.

You would have a hard time opening a pine cone, but for a crossbill it's easy. The bird simply pokes its bill into a pine cone and opens its mouth. Like magic, the hard scales of the pine cone are ripped away, uncovering the seeds inside. The bird then scoops up the seeds with its tongue, which is shaped a bit like a sugar scoop.

A guide to honey

In Africa there lives an animal known as a honey badger. As you might guess from its name, the honey badger likes honey. Whenever it finds a bee nest in a hollow tree or log, it breaks open the nest with its sharp claws, and gobbles up the honey. Because the badger has thick fur, even the stings of dozens of angry bees can't hurt it.

In a woods full of thousands of trees, the nests of wild bees can be hard to find. But the badger has a friend that helps it. This friend is a little bird known as a honeyguide.

Honeyguides, too, are fond of some of the things found inside a bee's nest. But they can't break open a nest as the badger can. So they have learned how to "talk" to the badgers and tell them where bee nests are! Then, when a badger breaks open a nest, the bird gets a share of the goodies.

Honeyguides are able to find bee nests easily because they are always watching for bees, which they eat. So, when one of the birds sees a honey badger, it tries to get the badger to follow it, while it looks for a nest. It attracts the badger's attention by darting back and forth and making a chattering sound. The badgers know what this sound means, and will follow the bird.

A honeyguide can usually find a bee nest in about half an hour. It then stops its chattering

The bird called a honeyguide leads animals such as the honey badger to honeybee nests.

and flies in little circles, showing where the nest is. It perches on a tree limb and waits while the badger opens up the nest and feasts. When the badger is finished, the bird goes into the nest to have a feast of wax and baby bees. Like the badgers, honeyguides aren't bothered by bee stings.

A honeyguide will also try to get a person to follow it to a bee nest. Africans who live near these birds gladly follow them to a reward of honey.

Other birds of the woods

Red-Shouldered Hawk

(North America)

Spruce Grouse

(North America)

Hawfinches
(Europe)

Red-Shafted Flicker
(Western North America)

Birds of Lakes, Rivers, and Swamps

A watery way of life

On a small lake in a northern part of the
world, a male Horned Grebe (greeb) is seeking
a mate. He swims about, singing his love
song—loud croaks, chattering sounds, and
shrieks! The lake echoes with noise, for there
are many grebes swimming in its bright
waters.

After a time, the male meets a female that
seems interested. He begins a "dance" to
attract her, and she joins him.

They face each other, then swim in a circle.
They shake their heads to show off their
"horns," the reddish-yellow plumes on each
side of the head. They touch their bills

**photographs
on pages 134–135**

Canada Geese on a
lake in Wyoming, and
a Horned Grebe

together, then dive down out of sight.
Moments later, they pop up again, each with a
clump of water plants in its bill. Then there is
more head-shaking and swimming in circles.
After a time, the two become mates.

A short time later, nest-building begins.
Grebes are strictly water birds. They can
hardly walk on land. Grebes need a nest they
can swim to. The nest they make is actually a
raft, floating on the water.

The two birds pick a shallow part of the
lake, where reeds and cattails are sticking up
out of the water. The birds dive down and
bring up billful after billful of dead plants
from the lake bottom. Working quickly, they
pile the soggy, muddy plants together to make
a large mound. The mound is fastened to the
stalk of a cattail.

When the nest is about one foot (30
centimeters) wide, the female grebe climbs on
top of it. She stomps and tramples with her
feet, to squeeze the material more tightly
together. Then she wiggles her body about to
form a shallow cup in the top of the nest. She
squats down in the cup. In time, she has laid
five eggs. She and her mate take turns sitting
on them.

The eggs hatch in about twenty-five days.
The babies are covered with grayish down,
striped and spotted with white. As soon as the
babies are dry, they take to the water, for
they can swim and dive right away. Even so,

they spend most of their time riding on their parents' backs. Even when the mother and father grebe dive for food, the little ones stay aboard.

But the babies soon begin to dart after insects, tadpoles, small frogs, and tiny fish themselves. As the young grebes become more and more able to care for themselves, the male grebe loses interest in them. Before long, he simply goes off on his own. However, the mother grebe stays with the young birds until they are fully grown.

By autumn, the grebes on the little lake no longer have the reddish-yellow plumes on each side of the head. These plumes are strictly

decorations for the mating season. But now it
is migration time. The grebes must leave soon,
before the lake begins to ice over and they
can no longer dive for food.

By ones and twos and small groups, the
grebes depart. They take off by actually
running a long way along the surface of the
water, flapping their wings until they finally
get into the air. Grebes are good fliers, but it
isn't easy for them to take off, so they only fly
when they must.

Horned Grebes live in North America and
in northern Europe and Asia. In Europe they
are known as Slavonian Grebes. There are a
number of different kinds of grebes. They are
all water birds, and their ways of life are
much the same.

Longlegs

A flamingo looks like a bird that someone made up! Its long, skinny, knobby-kneed legs look as if they should break under the bird's weight. Its long, thin neck can twist and turn into shapes a snake could never imitate!

But a flamingo's long legs and long neck are important to its way of life. A flamingo wades through the shallow water of a lake or lagoon to find its food. Its long legs keep its body up out of the water. But, with its long neck, the flamingo can reach far down into the water to get its food.

To eat, a flamingo holds its head upside down in the water—with the top of its head pointing downward. The bird keeps opening its mouth to let water in. Then it closes its mouth and squeezes the water out with its tongue. Each time, the tiny plants and animals in the water are trapped by tiny "strainers" inside the flamingo's mouth. The bird then swallows the trapped food.

Flamingo nests are mounds of mud that stick up out of shallow water. Female flamingos make these nests by heaping up mud they scrape off the lake bottom. At the top of the mound, the female scoops a shallow pit. In this, she lays one egg.

The female and her mate take turns incubating the egg for about a month, until it hatches. The baby flamingo is fed a sort of milky liquid that both the father and mother make in their throats.

Enormous flocks of flamingos are found in lakes and lagoons in Africa, Asia, South America, and southern Europe. There are four kinds of flamingos, all much alike. The biggest, the Greater Flamingo, is about four feet (1.2 meters) tall. Despite their long legs and long necks, flamingos are good swimmers. They are also good fliers. They usually fly in long lines, one after another.

flamingos

These Greater Flamingos of the West Indies are busy feeding in shallow water.

Snakebird

anhinga

After swimming, an anhinga must spread its wings to dry them. Even though the anhinga is a water bird, it has no oil in its feathers to make them waterproof.

In a warm southern swamp, a hungry bird hunts for food. It is a large, slim bird, a good three feet (0.9 meter) long. Swimming swiftly, with its long neck sticking up out of the water, it looks very much like a snake. No wonder it is often called a snakebird. It is also known as

a darter. And, for some unknown reason, people in the United States also call it a water turkey. But the true name of this bird is anhinga (an HIHNG guh).

After a time, the anhinga tilts its body and dives under water. Its strong feet propel it slowly and silently through the water. The long neck is now curved in the shape of an S as the bird peers from side to side in search of prey.

Suddenly, the anhinga sights a slow-swimming fish and glides toward it. Like a shot, the bird's neck snaps straight out. Its long, slim, needle-sharp bill stabs into the fish's body like a spear!

With the fish stuck on its bill, the anhinga swims to the surface. There, it gives a toss of its head, flipping the fish into the air. As the fish comes down, the bird catches it headfirst and swallows it whole.

The anhinga swims to a nearby bank and waddles up onto shore. It was graceful in the water, but on land it is clumsy and awkward. It spreads its wings to let them dry in the warm sunshine for a while. Then it flaps its wings and takes to the air. As it flies, it once again seems graceful.

Different kinds of anhingas live in swamps and along rivers and lakes in warm parts of the world. Besides fish, they also eat water snakes, and even small alligators—anything they can stab with their deadly bills.

The male Mandarin Duck (left) and the male Wood Duck (right) are two of the most beautifully colored of all the waterfowl.

Waterfowl

Ducks, geese, and swans are all related. They are all known as waterfowl, because they spend most of their time in lakes, ponds, rivers, or the sea. They all have webbed feet and are fine swimmers. Oil on their feathers makes them waterproof.

Swans are the giants of the waterfowl group. They are big birds, with long graceful necks. Some swans can stretch their necks to reach as high as a person's chest. Geese are smaller than swans, and have shorter necks. Ducks are smallest of all, and have the shortest necks.

You have probably heard or read that geese honk and ducks quack. That isn't quite true. Some geese do honk, but others make different sounds. Some cackle, much like a hen. Some cluck. And while many ducks do quack, many make a whistling noise. Wood ducks squeal, squeak, and cluck. And a male Redhead Duck *meows* like a cat!

As for swans, they, too, make several different kinds of noises. The call of a Trumpeter Swan sounds like a trumpet, or bugle. When a Mute Swan calls to its young ones, it sounds like a barking dog.

If you've ever seen a duck walk, you know that it waddles. This is because ducks have short, rather far-apart legs. Swans and most ducks are clumsy and awkward on land. Some kinds of ducks can barely walk at all, and hardly ever leave the water. Geese, which feed on land, are fairly good walkers.

Different kinds of waterfowl eat different things and have different ways of getting their food. Some kinds of ducks, such as Mallards, widgeons, and teals, are known as "dabbling" or "dipping" ducks. To get their food—water insects, snails, and water plants—they "duck" their heads underwater, with their feet and tails sticking straight up in the air. Swans feed this way, too, but they eat mostly plants.

Canvasback Ducks, Redheads, and several others, are known as diving ducks. They dive down and eat underwater. Their food is mostly water plants. However, there are some kinds of diving ducks that feed in the sea and eat mostly shellfish or fish.

Black Swan
(Australia and
New Zealand)

Burdekin Shelduck
(Australia)

Waterfowl of Australia and New Zealand

Pied Geese
(Australia)

Black, or Grey, Duck
(Australia and
New Zealand)

Blue-Billed Duck
(Australia)

Most kinds of geese get most of their food on land. They eat grass, seeds, and plants in meadows. Their bills can clip off the tops of plants as neatly as a pair of scissors.

Waterfowl also have several different ways of making nests. Swans make big, bulky piles of grass and water plants close to water. Both the male and female swans work to make the nest. Goose nests are much like swan nests, but only the female goose builds the nest. Some kinds of geese use nests made by other birds. They will even take over a nest in a tree, if the nest is big enough.

Most dabbling ducks nest on the ground. But the ducks known as perching ducks, which perch in trees, nest in holes in trees. And shelducks make their nests in rabbit holes and other animal burrows.

Before nest-building time, special feathers begin to grow on the breasts of female waterfowl. These very soft feathers are called nest-down. After the female has laid her eggs, she plucks these feathers with her bill and lines her nest with them. For hundreds of years people have collected nest-down feathers, especially from eider ducks. They use them to stuff pillows.

Baby waterfowl hatch with their eyes open and with down on their bodies. They can walk and swim right away. While the babies are growing up, first one parent and then the other molts, or sheds, the long wing and tail feathers. These are shed all at once, so that, for a short time, the birds cannot fly. During this time, the parent stays hidden in tall weeds. But by the end of summer, when the young ones are able to fly, both parents have new flight feathers. Thus, all the birds can migrate together.

When many kinds of waterfowl migrate, they fly in flocks that form patterns. Some,

Snow Geese

Mute Swans

Mute means "silent," and it is said that a Mute Swan does not use its voice in captivity. In Great Britain, the Mute Swan is considered a royal bird.

such as Canada Geese, fly in a pattern shaped like a V. Others, such as the geese known as Black Brants, may fly in a single, slanting line, one bird behind another. In this way, the leader, pushing through the air first, makes a "path" for the others. As one leader gets tired, another bird moves up to take its place.

Male, female, and baby waterfowl all have special names. A male duck is a drake, a female is a duck, and a baby is a duckling. A male goose is a gander, a female is a goose, and a baby is a gosling. A male swan is a cob, a female is a pen, and a baby is a cygnet (SIHG niht). A group of ducks or swans is called a flock, but a group of geese is often called—a gaggle!

Duck's Ditty

by Kenneth Grahame

All along the backwater,
Through the rushes tall,
Ducks are a-dabbling,
   Up tails all!

     Ducks' tails, drakes' tails,
     Yellow feet a-quiver,
     Yellow bills all out of sight
       Busy in the river!

         Slushy green undergrowth
         Where the roaches[1] swim—
         Here we keep our larder,[2]
           Cool and full and dim.

            Everyone for what he likes!
            We like to be
            Heads down, tails up,
              Dabbling free!

               High in the blue above
               Swifts whirl and call—
               We are down a-dabbling
                 Up tails all!

1. a kind of fish
2. food supply

The snail snatcher

It is early morning in a swamp in Florida. A grayish-brown bird with long legs and a white-speckled neck and back stands on a mudbank. It stands on one leg, with the other tucked up under its body. After a time, it puts this leg down and walks along the mudbank, toward the water. It seems to limp as it walks. This odd way of walking has given the bird its name—Limpkin.

The Limpkin wades into the shallow water. It moves along with its body just above the surface. Stretching its long neck down into the

Limpkin

A Limpkin uses its long bill to probe in the mud for snails.

water, it feels the muddy bottom with its long bill. After a time, it finds what it is looking for—a large snail, crawling in the mud. Using the tip of its bill like a pair of tweezers, the Limpkin picks up the snail and wades back to shore.

The snail is hiding inside its shell, of course, with the "door" tightly closed. But the Limpkin wedges the shell into a crack in a tree to hold it firmly, and waits. Before long, the snail feels safe enough to start coming out of the shell.

Jab! The Limpkin's bill stabs down. With a jerk of its head, the bird yanks the snail all the way out of the shell. It holds the snail in its bill for a while, as if it wants to enjoy the thought of the coming feast. Then, down goes the snail with a gulp!

Limpkins live in swamps and marshes in the Southeastern United States, Mexico, and Central and South America. They can swim well and can fly, but seldom do either. They wade in the water, searching for their favorite food, snails, and they perch in trees and run about among the branches.

A Limpkin nest is a loose pile of twigs, leaves and other bits of dead plants. Some Limpkins put their nest in a bush or tree, others build it in a clump of grass on the ground. A female Limpkin lays about six eggs. She and her mate take turns incubating them and caring for the young.

Hoatzins

A bird with "fingers"

Living along the banks of the big Amazon and
Orinoco rivers in South America are the
strange birds called Hoatzins (hoh AT sihnz).
These crow-sized birds live in small flocks of
ten or twenty. They eat the leaves of trees
that grow along the edges of the rivers. They
are the *only* birds that eat tree leaves.

The strangest thing about Hoatzins is that
the newborn chicks have little claws, or

"fingers," on their wings! Using their clawed fingers and their feet, the babies are like four-legged animals as they climb about in trees along the riverbanks. If something frightens a baby Hoatzin, it drops into the water and swims about, sometimes underwater, until the danger is past. Then, it climbs back into its tree.

Hoatzins soon lose their claws. And, as grown-ups, they never go into the water. Very poor fliers, they can fly only from one tree branch to another. They almost never go down to the ground.

A Hoatzin often eats so much that it gets top-heavy and has to prop itself up! Many birds have a kind of bag inside the neck, where they store the food they eat for a while before it goes to the stomach. This bag is called a crop. Hoatzins have a bigger crop than any other bird. A Hoatzin will eat until its crop is swollen and heavy with stored-up food. Then the bird has to lean on a branch and rest until it can move again!

baby Hoatzin

Young Hoatzins have little claws, like fingers, on their wings. These enable them to climb about in trees.

Lily trotters

The green circles of lily pads—thin, floating leaves—dot the blue water of a marsh in Mexico. Many small, long-legged birds are walking and trotting about on the lily pads. It might seem that each time a bird steps onto a pad, it would sink into the water. But these birds trot around as easily as if they were on solid ground!

These "unsinkable" birds are known as jaçanas (zhah suh NAHZ), or lily trotters. They have very large feet, with long, thin toes that are spread far apart. The toes spread out the bird's weight. There's not enough weight at any one place on either foot to push a lily pad down.

Thus, jaçanas live on top of the water. They walk and run about daintily, lifting each foot high. They jab their bills into the water to peck up water insects and seeds. Jaçanas can swim, but usually only do so if they feel they are in danger. They can also fly. But when danger is near, a jaçana often stands perfectly still. Its body blends in with the background, so that the bird is nearly invisible.

Among jaçanas, the female is the boss. It's the female who tries to get a male to be her mate, instead of the other way around. After she finds a mate and lays eggs, it's the male who incubates them and then takes care of the young ones. Baby jaçanas can run, dive,

jaçanas

These birds are also called lily trotters because they walk and run about on the tops of lily pads.

and swim the instant they hatch. They quickly learn to follow their father around on the lily pads.

There are a number of different kinds of jaçanas. All live in warm, southern parts of the world. The Australian lotus bird is one kind of jaçana.

A Belted Kingfisher in the act of swallowing a fish.

Kingfisher

A tiny fish swam close to the surface of a clear forest stream. On a tree branch sticking out over the stream sat a Belted Kingfisher, watching the water. When this expert fisher saw it, the fish was doomed!

Beak slightly open, the kingfisher swooped down over the water, dived in with a loud smack, and seized the startled fish. An instant later, the bird shot up out of the water and flew back to the branch. She banged the fish's head on the branch to stun it. Then she flipped the fish into the air and swallowed it headfirst.

Belted Kingfishers live mostly by themselves, near clear streams throughout North America. Each kingfisher has a territory that he or she will fiercely defend against any other kingfisher that tries to come into it!

However, in spring, pairs of kingfishers get together to mate and make a nest. Their nest is a long tunnel dug near the top of a steep riverbank. They work together, digging with their bills and using their feet to push the sand or mud out of the tunnel. It may take ten days of hard work for them to finish the job!

At the end of the tunnel, the kingfishers scoop out a large, round "room." No nest is made, but the dirt floor is soon littered with fishbones and scales. The female lays six or seven eggs on this bony carpet. The parents take turns incubating the eggs, which hatch in about twenty-four days.

Young kingfishers are able to fly in about four weeks, and leave the nest then. When they come out, they usually get a lesson in how to catch fish. One of their parents catches a fish, kills it, and sets it afloat in the water. The young birds practice diving at this target.

Different kinds of kingfishers live in many parts of the world. Despite their name, they don't all eat fish. The Kookaburra, a kingfisher of Australia, eats lizards, snakes, mice, crabs, and insects.

Other birds of lakes, rivers, and swamps

Crowned Crane

(Africa)

Shoebill Stork

(Africa)

American Bittern

(North America)

American Coot

(North and South America)

Common Egret

(North and South America,
Europe, Asia, Africa,
Australia)

Roseate Spoonbill

(North and South America)

Reddish Egret

(North and Central
America)

Snowy Egret

(North and South
America)

Birds of the Mountains

The giant glider

High above a mountainous part of southern California, a bird glides on outstretched wings. It is a very large bird, with a body as big as that of a young child. Its wings stretch a good ten feet (3 meters) from tip to tip. It is one of the largest of all flying birds—a California Condor.

The condor isn't a very pretty bird. Its body and wings are solid black, except for a snowy-white strip on the underside of each wing. It has no feathers on its wrinkled, yellowish-orange head and neck. Its eyes are bright red, and its ears are just holes surrounded by lumpy swirls of skin.

But the flight of the condor is graceful and beautiful. It soars, or glides, in vast, sweeping circles. It knows how to ride the currents of warm air that rise from the ground, so that it hardly ever has to flap its wings. The condor simply lets the air currents carry it along for miles.

**photographs
on pages 162–163**

Lammergeyer flying over mountaintops in Asia, and a California Condor

As the condor soars, it turns its wrinkled head from side to side, peering down at the rocky, forested land spread out below. It is seeking food. The condor is a flesh-eater, but it does not kill other creatures for its meals. It looks for an animal that is already dead. This is why it flies so high, in wide circles—so that it has a better chance of seeing a dead animal on the ground below.

Even though it may fly great distances each day in its search for food, a condor isn't always able to find something to eat. It must sometimes go for days without eating. But, today it is in luck. It spies a large, brown form lying in a brushy canyon—a deer that was wounded by a hunter, but managed to run a long way before it died.

The condor needs a big animal such as a deer, sheep, or cow, for it can eat about two pounds (0.9 kilogram) of meat at a time. However, it will gladly eat smaller creatures, too, such as dead squirrels, rabbits, and even fish. But it does not care for the meat of any creature that has been dead for too long. It prefers fresh meat.

The condor descends cautiously, in broad, slow circles. Finally, it lands, coming to a rather clumsy, running stop. A cluster of ravens had been pecking at the deer's body. But, as the condor approaches, they quickly flap away. They have no wish to argue over food with this giant bird!

The condor paces forward in stately fashion,
much like a strutting turkey. Bending down, it
slices into the deer's skin and muscle with its
strong, sharp beak.

Before long, other condors start arriving to
share the feast. Watching with keen eyes as
they soared on high, they had seen the first
condor glide down. This told them food had
been found. Soon, half a dozen of the big birds
surround the deer. They share peaceably,
with only an occasional squabble breaking out
when two happen to want the same tidbit!

In time, the first condor has eaten its fill.
Turning away, the bird leans forward and rubs
its head and neck on the grass to clean itself.

The condor's way of eating is the reason why it has no feathers on its head and neck. It often has to push its head down into the bloody inside of a dead animal. Feathers on its head and neck would get dirty and bloody, so nature has seen to it that the bird has none. Bare skin is easier to clean.

Many people dislike condors, vultures, and other birds that eat dead creatures. But these

birds do a very useful and important job. They help to get rid of the world's garbage! They start the work of disposing of a dead animal by opening up its body. Other creatures—birds, animals, insects, and tiny microscopic creatures—then do their part. Slowly, the animal's body vanishes.

The condor finishes cleaning itself and decides to take to the air again. But, for these birds, it isn't as easy to take off from the ground as it is from a cliff or a high tree. The condor has to run along clumsily, half-hopping and flapping its wings before it finally rises into the air. But then its clumsiness vanishes. Once again, it becomes a graceful glider.

Looking at a California Condor is like looking more than ten thousand years into the past! These birds shared the world with creatures that no longer exist—huge bison, giant sloths the size of an elephant, and woolly mammoths. The condors are leftover prehistoric animals.

But, sadly, the California Condors are dying out. In past years, people have shot and poisoned many of these birds. People have even stolen their eggs. And a condor lays only one egg every two years. Now, there are probably no more than twenty or thirty California Condors left in the world. Attempts have been made to save them, but it may be too late. These marvelous birds may soon be extinct.

Golden Eagle

The king of birds

In a narrow valley in the mountains, a rabbit hopped through the underbrush. It did not notice the winged shape circling overhead. But, keen eyes looking down saw the rabbit.

Slowly, the winged shape circled lower. It was a big bird with a yellowish-brown body and golden feathers on the back of its head and neck. A Golden Eagle.

When the eagle was about three hundred feet (90 meters) above the rabbit, it folded its wings. Like a thunderbolt (a flash of lightning), it dived headfirst at tremendous speed. At the last instant, its wings snapped open and one foot reached out. The three toes on the foot were tipped with curved, razor-sharp claws. The claws stabbed into the rabbit, killing it so quickly that it never knew what happened.

With the dead rabbit clutched in its foot, the eagle skimmed upward. On a cliff ledge high on a mountainside was a huge, bulky nest made of tree branches. In it, two hungry baby eagles waited. This eagle was their father. He would bring the rabbit to the nest. There, the mother eagle would tear it to pieces with her sharp, hooked beak. She would carefully feed thin shreds of meat to the babies.

Often called the "king of birds," the Golden Eagle is a swift, powerful, and graceful flier. It is a skillful hunter, and a bird of great courage. When it is really hungry, it will attack deer and other animals much larger than itself. However, it usually hunts mostly rabbits, ground squirrels, and other small animals.

Golden Eagles live mostly in mountainous parts of North America, Scotland, Sweden and Norway, and northern Asia. In some places, farmers and ranchers kill these birds because they believe the eagles prey on lambs. But to many people, the Golden Eagle is a symbol of freedom, to be admired and protected.

The Eagle

By Alfred, Lord Tennyson

He clasps the crag with crooked hands;
Close to the sun in lonely lands,
Ringed with the azure world, he stands.

The wrinkled sea beneath him crawls;
He watches from his mountain walls,
And like a thunderbolt he falls.

The bone eater

If you were asked, "What creature eats bones?", you'd probably answer, "A dog." But there's also a *bird* that eats bones. It lives in the mountains of Africa, southern Europe, and central Asia. It is the Lammergeyer (LAM uhr geye uhr), or Bearded Vulture.

The Lammergeyer is a big bird. Its body is four feet (1.2 meters) long. Its wings stretch about nine feet (2.7 m) from one wing tip to the other. It soars over the mountain peaks and valleys, peering down in search of the bodies of dead creatures. Sometimes it waits, patiently, while vultures eat the flesh of a dead sheep or other animal. When they leave, the Lammergeyer goes down to feast on the leftovers.

The Lammergeyer eats a lot of dead meat. It can also swallow small bones, whole. It takes large bones in its beak and, flying high into the air, drops them so that they shatter on the rocks below. Then it flies down and munches them up, especially to get at the marrow, the soft part inside.

Lammergeyers build huge nests inside caves or on cliff ledges. The nests are made of tree branches, bones, and animal skins.

Lammergeyer

A Peregrine Falcon
with a pigeon it has
killed.

A hunter in the sky

Like the Golden Eagle, the bird called a
Peregrine (PEHR uh grihn) Falcon is a hunter.
But instead of hunting for animals that live on
the ground, a Peregrine Falcon hunts and
catches other birds in midair.

A Peregrine Falcon is a *very* fast flier. It can
catch most small birds, such as jays or crows,
even if they have a long head start. It grabs
them with a clawed foot, in a grip that kills
them instantly.

For larger birds, such as ducks, the falcon has a different way of hunting. It dives from a great height, moving at tremendous speed—up to 180 miles (290 kilometers) an hour! The falcon strikes with its clawed toes, killing its prey at once.

As the dead bird falls toward the ground, the falcon may swoop after it, nimbly catching it with one foot before it hits the ground. Or, the falcon may circle up and around and follow the bird down to the ground.

Before a Peregrine Falcon eats its kill, it uses its beak to pull out most of the dead bird's feathers. Then, holding the bird with one foot, it tears off strips of meat with its hooked beak.

Peregrine Falcons make their nests high up on the ledges of cliffs or in holes in the sides of cliffs. The nest is nothing but a shallow pit that the female falcon scrapes out with her claws. She lays three or four eggs that have reddish-brown splotches and speckles.

In the 1960's, human pollution caused a kind of poisoning that nearly wiped out the Peregrine Falcons in North America and Europe. But some scientists managed to raise healthy birds in laboratories. These birds were turned loose to breed, and seem to be surviving. Even the number of wild birds is increasing again. There is hope that these swift hunters of the sky will once more become plentiful.

An underwater hunter

High up on a mountainside a small waterfall plunged over the edge of a cliff. It fell some sixty feet (18 meters), sending up a cloud of spray and making a loud, hissing roar. From the base of the waterfall, a clear, cold stream rushed down the mountainside.

On a rock in the middle of the stream, not far from the waterfall, perched a small, stocky bird. It bobbed its head, flicked its tail, and sang a sweet, twittering song. Then it walked into the icy, rushing water.

The bird dived down to the bottom of the stream. Using its wings as paddles, it swam along just above the bottom. Then it spied a little crawling creature that looked like a caterpillar with six legs. Snatching the insect in its bill, the bird swam back to the surface.

This bird that hunts in rushing mountain streams is called a dipper. Dippers live in mountains in most parts of the world. Their favorite territory is rocks drenched with the spray of a roaring waterfall. They will even build their nest in a rocky hollow behind a waterfall—so that they must fly through the water to get to and from the nest.

Dippers get most of their food underwater. They feed mostly on the larvae, or babies, of stone flies, caddis flies, and mayflies, which live underwater. But dippers will also gladly eat small fish. And they'll snatch up adult caddis flies and other insects that they find on the banks of streams.

Dippers are specially equipped for living as they do. Besides upper and lower eyelids, they have a third eyelid that is transparent. This eyelid keeps out the water when the birds are walking or flying in heavy spray. When they go into the water, a special flap covers their nostrils to keep the water out. And a very large preen gland provides oil to keep their feathers waterproof.

Despite these differences, dippers are really just perching birds. They are closely related to robins, sparrows, and starlings. But of all the many perching birds, dippers are the only ones that have learned to move about in the water.

Dipper
The birds known as dippers hunt for most of their food at the bottom of swift mountain streams.

Other birds
of the mountains

Himalayan Monal

(Asia)

Alpine Chough

(Europe)

Kea

(New Zealand)

Birds of the Jungle

Artistic birds

In a dense forest in Australia, a bird was hard at work, building something. The bird had already made a sort of thick "carpet" of woven twigs on the ground. Now, using its bill, it jammed other twigs into the carpet so that they stood upright. In went one twig after another, until there was a long wall.

Then the bird built another wall of twigs across from the first. The two walls enclosed a narrow path just wide enough for the bird to walk through.

The bird flew off. It was back shortly, with some charcoal in its bill. It chewed the charcoal into a black paste. Then it picked up a piece of bark in its bill. Using the bark like a sponge, the bird swabbed the black "paint" on the insides of the walls of twigs!

**photographs
on pages 180–181**

Hoatzins in a tropical forest, and a Satin Bowerbird

When this decorating was done, the bird flew off again. It returned carrying a blue flower. Carefully, the bird placed the flower on the carpet in front of the walls of twigs. Then it stepped back with its head cocked to one side. It seemed to be trying to decide if it had put the flower in the right place!

Apparently, it didn't think it had. It stepped forward and moved the flower. Then it flew off again. Some time later, it returned. This time, it had a shiny blue wing of a beetle. This, too, it placed on the carpet of twigs.

The bird went back and forth like this for the rest of the day. Each time it returned, it brought a new decoration—a berry, another flower, a bird feather, and even the plastic cover of a ball-point pen. Most of these things were blue, but one was yellow. Each was placed on the carpet.

Finally, the bird was finished. It flew up into a nearby tree and began to sing.

A structure made of leafy branches is called a bower. So, this kind of bird is known as a bowerbird. And because its shiny blue feathers look like the shiny cloth called satin, the bird is known as a Satin Bowerbird.

Why does this bird make its painted walls and carpet of twigs, and decorate them with objects? Actually, only male bowerbirds do such work. They use their bowers as a sort of stage to attract female bowerbirds at mating time.

When a female bird sees the bower, she will
usually come to it. Immediately, the male
steps "onstage" and begins to act. He
stretches his neck, opens his wings, spreads
out his tail, and sings. If the female is
charmed, she becomes his mate!

Different kinds of bowerbirds make different kinds of bowers—large domes, pyramids, tunnels, and arches. All of these birds decorate their bowers with such things as snail shells, glittery beetle wings, colorful berries, flowers, and stones. They even use bits of glass, paper, cloth, bottle caps, and other things people have left lying about. Several kinds of bowerbirds also paint their bowers, as the satin bowerbird does.

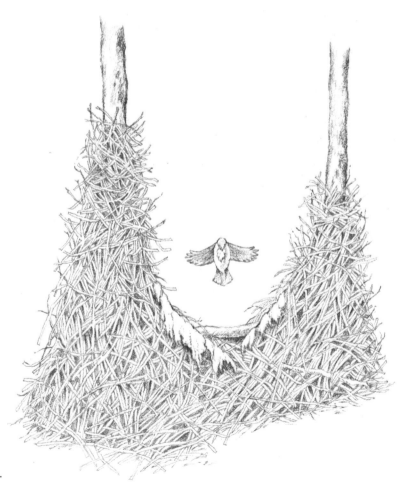

The bower of a
Golden Bowerbird.

The bower of a
Gardener Bowerbird.

Bowerbirds live in Australia and on the
nearby island of New Guinea. They eat fruit,
berries, and insects. Some of the bowers they
make are so fancy that it's hard to imagine
birds made them. The first explorers to see a
bowerbird's work thought the bower had been
built by people.

Big, bright bills

Toucans are famous for their big, bright bills.
There are about forty different kinds of
toucans, and they all have large, long, brightly
colored bills. Some toucans have a bill nearly
as long as their whole body. Although these
bills look heavy, they aren't. The inside of the
bill is like a honeycomb, with many hollow
places, making it quite light. The outside is a
thin, tough shell that provides strength.

Most birds' bills are special tools that help
the birds get certain kinds of food. But a
toucan could get its food just as easily with a
much smaller bill. No one knows for sure why
these birds have such big, bright bills.

Toucans live in warm, wet forests from

Keel-Billed Toucans

Mexico to Argentina. They live by themselves or in flocks of up to a dozen birds. They hop about in the top branches of the trees, plucking berries and fruits with the tips of their bills. They also snap up spiders, insects, and small birds, especially if they find baby birds in a nest.

Toucans are playful creatures. They often play catch with fruits and berries. With its bill, one bird will toss a berry into the air, and another will catch it. Toucans also have "duels" that seem almost playful, in which they use their bills like swords!

Common Potoo

Hidden in plain sight

Night is falling in a forest in southern Mexico. As the sun sets, the forest grows dark. Suddenly, a broken branch on a tree limb seems to come to life! A pair of yellow eyes appears on it! The "branch" spreads a pair of wings and flies away!

The bird known as a potoo (poh TOO) spends its days sitting upright on the end of a broken branch with its bill pointed toward the sky. It keeps its eyes nearly closed, holds itself stiff, and never moves. Its shape and color make it look like part of the branch. Even though it is out in plain sight, it is completely hidden from its enemies.

At night, a potoo leaves its special branch and flies to another tree. There it perches, peering into the darkness for fat flying insects. When it spies one, it darts into the air and grabs the insect in its wide mouth. Then it flies back to its perch to watch and wait again.

Potoos don't build nests. A female potoo simply lays a single egg on the top of a broken branch. She and her mate take turns sitting on the egg until it hatches. The birds are safe because they look like part of the tree, and the egg is safe because it's hidden under them.

When the baby potoo hatches, it is covered with white down. Whenever its parents leave it alone while they go hunting, it stays stiff and motionless on the branch. It looks just like a kind of mushroom that often grows on trees. Thus, both young and adult potoos can "hide" in plain sight.

A female potoo lays her egg on the top of a broken branch.

Jungle runner

The big birds called cassowaries (KAS uh wehr eez) live in forests in northern Australia, New Guinea, and nearby islands. They cannot fly, but they can run fast. Even in a thick forest a cassowary can move as fast as thirty miles (48 kilometers) an hour. And it can jump as high as six feet (1.8 meters) to leap over logs and bushes.

These birds look as if they have no wings. Actually, their wings are just very small, and hidden by a lot of feathers. But cassowaries have a use for their wings, even though they don't fly. As a cassowary walks through the thick forest, it holds out its little wings to push away thorns and vines. It also stretches out its neck so that the bony helmet on its head will push aside branches.

Cassowaries eat mostly seeds, fruits, and berries, but they also gobble up small animals if they have the chance. They are good swimmers, and will sometimes plunge into a river to chase and catch fish. They hunt their food in early morning and late afternoon, when it's coolest. The rest of the day, each bird rests in a sunny clearing it has found for itself.

Cassowaries live by themselves most of the time. But at the beginning of their mating season, pairs of them get together and build a nest. They make a big untidy pile of leaves and sticks at the foot of a tree. The female lays from three to six blotchy green eggs that blend into the leaves of the nest. The male incubates the eggs until they hatch. And it is he who cares for the young birds until they can look after themselves.

There are several kinds of cassowaries. The biggest kind is about five feet (1.5 m) tall and weighs as much as 120 pounds (54 kilograms).

cassowaries

Cave birds

Deep in a South American rain forest is a
large cave. Inside this cave it is as black as
pitch. In the blackness there is constant
noise—screeches, wails, and clicking sounds.
Up near the roof of the cave, many creatures
are flying. They turn and wheel swiftly in the
darkness. Never once do they bump into one
another, or into the rocky walls or ceiling.

What are these creatures? Bats live in
caves, and can fly in darkness without
bumping into anything. Are these creatures
bats? No, they are Oilbirds—birds that are
very much like bats. For, like bats, these birds
have a kind of sonar system in their bodies.
They use *sounds* to "see" their way in
darkness.

As an Oilbird flies about in the cave, it

makes clicking sounds. The sounds shoot out ahead of it. If the sounds strike something, they come bouncing straight back. The bird's ears pick up these returning sounds. From these echoes, the bird can tell that something is ahead of it. It can even tell how big the thing is, and how far away! Thus, the Oilbird can fly through the cave at top speed, without bumping into things.

By day, Oilbirds rest on ledges in their cave. At night, they fly out into the forest to feed. Outside the cave, they don't need their "sonar." Like owls, they can see in darkness as long as there is some moonlight or starlight. All night the Oilbirds hover among the trees, plucking palm-tree fruits and eating them as they fly. Before morning they go streaming back to their dark caves.

These birds are called Oilbirds because they have a lot of oil in their bodies. Baby Oilbirds are fed the same rich, oily palm fruits their parents eat. So they grow very, very plump! Before they can fly, they weigh almost twice as much as the older birds.

The most beautiful birds

In the forests of New Guinea live the most beautiful of all birds. When some of their feathers were first brought to Europe, people thought such birds must be from paradise, or heaven. Thus, the birds became known as birds of paradise.

There are about forty different kinds of birds of paradise. A few kinds are not very colorful, but most are. Some of these birds almost look as if they are wearing costumes!

King Bird of Paradise

Lesser Bird of Paradise

At mating time, the males show off their bright colors and fancy feathers to attract females. The males spread their wings and tails or raise their head, neck, or body feathers to form fantastic ruffles and crowns. Then they twist, turn, and dance to charm a female into mating with them.

Often, many male birds of paradise perform at the same time on nearby perches in the treetops. Females watch these performances and choose the best dancer as their mate.

Blue Bird of Paradise
As part of its mating dance, this bird hangs upside down.

Wilson's Bird of Paradise

King of Saxony
Bird of Paradise

Six-Wired Bird
of Paradise

The terror of the treetops

The Harpy Eagle is the terror of the treetops in the forests of Central and South America! It is the largest of all eagles. This bird hunts monkeys, sloths, and other large tree-dwelling animals. At times, it dives down to the forest floor to seize a small, ratlike agouti (uh GOO tee). It may also swoop down near a human community to snatch up a young pig, or even a dog!

Harpy Eagles are fast fliers. They speed through a forest in short spurts, stopping to perch on trees to look and listen for prey. A Harpy Eagle seizes its prey with a killing grip of its clawed feet.

Most of the time, a Harpy Eagle lives by itself. But at mating season, pairs of these eagles get together and build nests high in the tops of tall trees. When their eggs hatch, both the male and female eagles go hunting food for their young ones.

Harpy Eagles are named for the Harpies in Greek mythology. Harpies were said to be fierce, savage beings with the head of a hideous witch and the wings, legs, and body of a bird of prey.

The Harpy Eagle was named after the Harpy, a mythical creature with the head of a witch and the body of a bird.

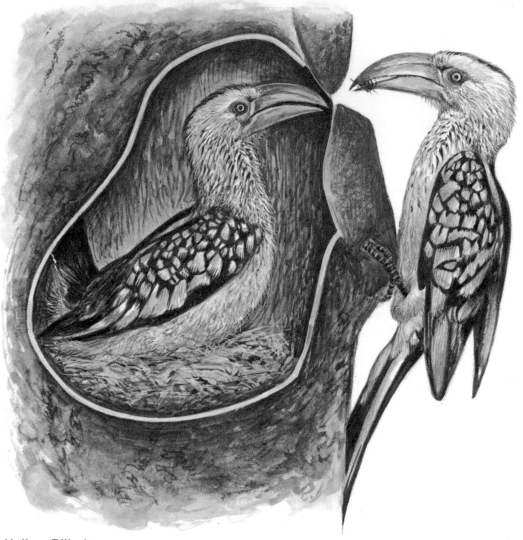

**Yellow-Billed
Hornbills**

"Jailbirds"

When a female African hornbill is ready to lay eggs, she puts herself in "jail"! And there her babies hatch and grow up!

At egg-laying time, a female hornbill looks for a tree with a hole in it—like a little cave. With the help of her mate, she begins building a wall across the hole's entrance. The wall is made mostly of mud. The nest is made during a rainy time, so there is plenty of mud around.

While the male hornbill brings billfuls of mud, the female builds the wall. She works from inside the hole, so that slowly, she walls herself in. Finally, the entrance is completely covered, except for a narrow slit in the middle. The mud dries hard as rock, and there's the female hornbill—in "jail"!

Once the hornbill walls herself in, she and her babies are safe from snakes, monkeys, and other creatures. Of course, she and the babies have to eat, and that's why the narrow slit was left in the wall. The male hornbill brings fruit or insects and feeds them to his family through the hole. He spends most of his time bringing food to the walled-up nest.

When the babies are about half grown, the mother hornbill breaks out of her jail by battering down the wall with her bill. However, as soon as she is out, the *babies* start to rebuild the wall! They, too, leave a narrow slit through which their mother and father can feed them. They stay "jailbirds" until they are ready to fly. Then they and their parents break down the wall again.

There are a number of different kinds of hornbills. They generally live in flocks in the hot forests of Africa and parts of Asia. Some hornbills are no more than fifteen inches (37.5 centimeters) long. Others are nearly as big as a turkey.

The parrot family

As everyone knows, parrots are birds that can "talk." They can also do perfect imitations of many sounds, such as a whistle, a squeaking door, and so on.

Wild parrots don't talk and don't imitate things. They just screech and squawk. But tame parrots that live among people grow fond of them and may try to attract attention by making sounds such as humans make. A number of other kinds of birds, such as crows and mynas, can also be taught to talk. But when a parrot or any other bird says words, it doesn't really *understand* what it is saying. It is just making noises to attract attention.

One of the kinds of parrots that people most often keep as a pet, and teach to speak, is the Blue-Fronted Parrot. These parrots live in large flocks in the forests of South America. There, they fly and climb about looking for trees with good fruit, nuts, and seeds. When a parrot finds a likely fruit or nut, it first tastes the food with its thick tongue to make sure the food is good to eat.

Besides getting all their food from trees, these parrots also make their nests in holes in trees. Because they spend so much time moving about in trees, they are good climbers. They use their feet and bill to grasp branches and pull themselves about.

A number of different kinds of parrots live

Blue-Fronted Parrot

in the South American forests. So do the birds called macaws, which are members of the parrot family. All these birds live in much the same way. Many of them are brightly colored. Strange as it may seem, their coloring may actually help to hide them from enemies. When they sit among the leaves of a tree, they look like a bright flower or fruit.

Scarlet Macaws and Red-and-Green Macaws

Pink Cockatoo

African Gray Parrot

Several other kinds of parrots live in forests in Africa. One of these is the African Gray Parrot, which also makes a good pet that can be taught to speak.

Many members of the parrot family live in Australia and Asia. The birds known as cockatoos, lorikeets, lories, parakeets, and budgerigars are all parrots.

Rainbow Lorikeet

Other birds of the jungle

Kaka
(New Zealand)

Blue-Crowned Motmot
(Central and South America)

Masked Lovebirds
(Africa)

Hill Myna
(Asia)

Victoria Crowned Pigeon
(New Guinea)

Birds of the Desert

212

The speedy snake killer

The rattlesnake was ready to strike! It had its head lifted and drawn back. Its jaws were stretched wide open. Its yellow eyes glared at the large, rather awkward-looking bird that faced it. The rattler was young and small, but its bite would still kill the bird instantly. And the snake could strike in the blink of an eye!

The bird, however, seemed unafraid. It circled the snake swiftly, forcing the snake to swing around to follow it. Suddenly, the bird made a lightning-fast lunge at the snake. At once, the snake struck!

photographs on pages 210–211

sandgrouse gathered at a waterhole in Africa, and a Roadrunner

But—the bird wasn't there. The lunge was a trick. At the last instant, the bird dodged. The snake missed its strike and fell full-length on the ground. In a flash, the bird darted in. With its long, pointed bill, the bird hammered the snake's skull until the reptile was dead. Then the bird calmly picked the snake up in its bill and slowly swallowed it, headfirst!

This bird that preys so fearlessly upon poisonous snakes is the Roadrunner. It's a good-sized bird, with a body about a foot (30 centimeters) long and a slim, straight tail that's just about as long as its body. Roadrunners are found in the deserts and dry parts of southwestern North America. They got their name because they are often seen running along roads.

Snakes are only one of the many things that Roadrunners eat. Mostly, they eat grasshoppers, big tarantula spiders, and scorpions. They'll also happily feast on lizards, toads, mice, smaller birds, and bird eggs, as well as some seeds and fruit.

A Roadrunner kills a snake by hammering the snake's head with its bill. But it kills most other creatures in a different way. It holds the animal in its bill and pounds the animal's head against a handy rock!

Most of the creatures a Roadrunner hunts can move quite quickly. The bird has to be fast to catch them—and it is. A Roadrunner can run at an average speed of fifteen miles

(2.4 kilometers) an hour. Some Roadrunners have even been timed at twenty-six miles (4.1 km) an hour. That's much faster than any human can run.

Roadrunners are also spry and alert. They can turn, twist, and change direction in an instant. They can easily follow any prey that's trying to dodge away. And they are cunning—they sometimes lie in wait at drinking places and seize birds that fly down for a drink.

Of course, a Roadrunner doesn't really run all the time. Much of the time it just walks at a fairly fast pace. But a Roadrunner hardly ever flies. Indeed, it cannot fly very well. Only if it is frightened, or being chased, will it take to the air. Even then, it never goes more than about ten feet (3 meters) off the ground, and it comes down again very quickly.

When a pair of Roadrunners mates, the female builds the nest. She weaves twigs into a sort of shallow basket in a cactus, bush, or small tree. She lines the basket with grass, leaves, or other soft material.

In this nest, the female lays from two to twelve eggs. She lays one egg every other day. Thus, some eggs hatch ahead of others. A Roadrunner nest often contains several unhatched eggs, some small, weak babies, and perhaps an older, stronger youngster beginning to grow feathers.

Roadrunners feed their babies the same things they eat—often stuffing lizards headfirst down the youngsters' throats! Usually, the lizards are bigger than the babies. Their long tails will hang out of the babies' mouths for hours until the babies can swallow the rest of their huge meal!

Flying sponges

Most of the Kalahari Desert of southern Africa is as dry as an old bone. Only in a few places along its edges are there some small, shallow ponds filled with rainwater.

Each day, at dawn and at dusk, big crowds of birds fly out of the desert. They are sandgrouse, looking for water. Some kinds of desert birds get water by eating insects that have a lot of water in their bodies. But sandgrouse eat only seeds. They must have water to drink. So, once or twice a day, the birds fly to a pond. This may mean a flight of as much as thirty miles (50 kilometers).

The birds glide down near the edge of a pond. After waiting and watching for a few minutes to make sure all is safe, they walk to the water. They plunge their bills in and drink deeply. They must drink enough water to last them all day or all night.

When they are finished drinking, the male birds wade deeper into the water. They kneel and wiggle their bodies. It looks as if they are taking a bath—but that isn't what they are doing. They are deliberately soaking their breast feathers, which hold water like a sponge.

Each male sandgrouse soaks up as much water as it can. Then the birds take off for the long flight back into the desert. About half the water in a male's feathers dries up on the way.

These birds are a pair of Double-Banded Sandgrouse. The one on the left is a male. The other is a female.

But there is still quite a bit left by the time the birds reach "home."

A male flies to the place where his three or four babies have been waiting. He stands with his chest puffed out. The baby birds nibble and suck at his feathers, drinking the water he has brought for them. The little birds can't yet fly to get their own water—so their father becomes a "flying sponge" and takes it to them!

A desert homebuilder

In some of the deserts of southwestern North America there lives a sort of "official homebuilder" for many of the desert creatures. It's the bird known as the Gila (HEE luh) Woodpecker.

Most woodpeckers make their nests by boring holes in tree trunks. However, there are few if any trees in the southwestern deserts. But there *are* giant cactus plants that grow as tall as a tree and as thick as a

A Gila Woodpecker feeding on a cactus.

telephone pole. The woodpeckers make their nests in these cactus plants.

A giant cactus is covered with millions of hard, sharp needles. The needles keep animals from biting into the plant to get at its soft, juicy inside. But a Gila Woodpecker's tough little toes don't feel the prick of the needles. And the woodpecker's sharp bill cuts into the soft cactus as easily as a knife cuts into cheese.

High up on the side of a giant cactus, a Gila Woodpecker will bore a hole about two inches (5 centimeters) wide and from nine to sixteen inches (22-40 cm) deep. Sap begins to ooze out of the sides of this hole. As the sap hardens, it makes the sides of the hole hard and smooth. The female lays her eggs in the hole, and the babies hatch and grow up there.

When the young birds are old enough to fly, the whole woodpecker family leaves the nest. But the nest doesn't stay empty very long. A great many kinds of desert birds and animals will gladly move into an old Gila Woodpecker hole in a giant cactus. Cactus wrens, martins, several kinds of owls, and other birds often take over Gila Woodpecker nests. So do snakes, lizards, and sometimes even desert rats and mice.

Thus, the Gila Woodpecker is truly a desert homebuilder. A great many desert creatures seem to depend upon this bird for their dwelling places.

The Gibber Bird

Some parts of Australia are covered with
millions of small, round, smooth stones. The
stones are known as gibbers (JIHB uhrz), and
the areas of land are called gibber plains.

A gibber plain is just about the most bare
and desolate kind of desert there is. It is
waterless, and gets sizzling hot in summer.
And yet, a small bird called a Gibber Bird, or
Gibber Chat, makes this hot, stony desert its
home.

Why would a bird live in such a place?
Mainly because there is plenty of food for it.
A gibber plain swarms with insects that love
such hot, dry places. The Gibber Bird runs
about over the stones, snapping up insects as
it goes. It hardly ever flies.

There are also plenty of seeds for a Gibber

Bird to find and eat. It seldom rains on a gibber plain, but when it does, millions of plants sprout from seeds lying among the stones. The plants grow quickly in the bright, hot sunshine. They soon die, but first they produce billions of seeds. These make new plants after the next rainfall. As for water, a Gibber Bird gets what water it needs from the seeds and insects it eats.

In the hottest days of summer, a Gibber Bird finds the coolest, shadiest place it can, such as a hole dug by a lizard. There the bird stays, hardly moving. In this way, it conserves, or saves up, the energy and moisture in its body.

All this may seem like a hard life, but Gibber Birds seem perfectly content to live as they do. The gibber desert is their home, and they never leave it.

This Elf Owl has taken over an old nest that
a Gila Woodpecker made in a giant cactus.

A desert elf

It is dusk on a desert in the American Southwest. A giant cactus stands outlined against the setting sun. High up on the side of the cactus, yellow eyes gleam from a small hole. A tiny Elf Owl, the size of a sparrow, stares into the gathering darkness.

During the day, the Elf Owl had stayed hidden in its cactus home. Now, at dusk, it comes out and begins to call to others of its kind. The yips and whistles of the little owls resound through the desert. For such small creatures, Elf Owls have very loud voices!

A beetle drones through the dusk, flying toward the cactus. The owl shoots out of its hole. With one clawed foot, it snatches the beetle out of the air!

Nighttime is hunting time for Elf Owls. Like all owls, they prey upon live animals. But because Elf Owls are so small, they must hunt small prey, such as flying insects, which they grab in midair. They also snatch up little creatures off the ground—crickets, scorpions, grasshoppers, and small snakes and lizards.

Throughout the night, the little bird hunts. With the approach of dawn, it heads back to its nest—a nest it has taken over from a Gila Woodpecker, for these little owls never make a nest of their own. The little Elf Owl pops inside and settles down to rest during the long, hot day that is about to begin.

Other birds of the desert

Gambel's Quail
(North America)

Houbara Bustard
(Africa, Asia)

Cactus Wren

(North America)

Birds of the Sea and Shore

A big-mouthed bird

A wonderful bird is the pelican!
His beak holds more than his belican.

> from *The Pelican Chorus*
> by Edward Lear

photographs
on pages 226–227

gulls at the seashore
in California, and a
Brown Pelican

It's probably true that a pelican's bill can hold
more than its belly can. The underside of a
pelican's lower bill is a piece of loose, rubbery
skin. It stretches and swells to form a big
pouch that can hold as much as three and a
half gallons (13.3 liters) of water!

Many people think a pelican uses its big throat pouch for storing fish, but that isn't true. A pelican's bill is a "scoop" for *catching* fish.

When a hungry pelican sees a fish swimming near the surface of the sea, it dives into the water and opens its mouth. Its pouch scoops up a large amount of water, as well as the fish. The bird shoots up to the surface and tips its head down to let the water drain out of its pouch. Then it lifts its head and swallows the fish.

Pelicans known as Brown Pelicans live along the coasts of southern North America, South America, and on nearby islands. They are big birds, about as tall as a young child. Stretched straight out, their wings spread six and a half feet (1.9 meters). These birds look funny waddling about on land, but they are graceful gliders and fliers.

Brown Pelicans like to live in groups. During the mating season, they may gather by the thousands. Where there are plenty of trees, they make their nests in treetops. Where trees are few, the nests are made on the ground. Brown Pelican nests are made of piles of twigs, leaves, and grass.

A mother pelican lays from one to four eggs. At first, the babies are weak and helpless. Their eyes are closed and they have no feathers. But after a few days they are strong enough to poke their heads into their parents' pouches for food. The parents squirt up bits of fish out of their stomachs for the babies to eat.

As the babies get older, feeding time is often wild and noisy! For, when pelicans nest on the ground, the babies soon leave the nests to form large "gangs." When a grown-up pelican appears, all the young ones come charging at it in the hope of getting food. Sometimes, the grown-up actually has to run away! But most of the time it just pushes through the noisy crowd until it finds its own babies and feeds them.

For a long time, Brown Pelicans were in

trouble. Scientists feared they might all be killed by pollution. This hasn't happened, but there is still danger. Pelicans are also in danger because people catch more and more of the kind of fish pelicans eat. If too much of their food is taken, they will die off.

There are several other kinds of pelicans, some of which aren't sea birds. They live near swamps and river mouths in Africa, Europe, and Australia. Many of these birds catch fish by poking their head underwater while swimming, not by diving like the Brown Pelican. Otherwise, their ways of life are very much alike.

Whale birds

Have you ever heard of a whale bird? It's not a bird that's as *big* as a whale, of course! It's a bird that got its nickname because it follows whales. Its real name is Red (or Gray) Phalarope (FAL uh rohp). This bird will fly above a whale, or even come down to perch on the big animal's back!

Red Phalaropes follow whales because the huge animals stir up many small sea creatures. These creatures come to the surface of the water, where the phalaropes can catch them easily. The phalaropes land on a whale's back to search for small, shrimplike creatures that fasten themselves to a whale's body.

Red Phalaropes following a Killer Whale.

Red Phalaropes, or Gray Phalaropes as they are called in Europe, live over or on the water most of their lives. They spend all winter at sea, in the southern half of the world. During the winter months, their feathers are gray and white.

But for a little more than a month of each year, Red Phalaropes become land birds. They migrate to the tundra, the great icy plains of the Far North. Now, during the summer months, their feathers are mostly red and brown. While the tundra blooms with plants and buzzes with insects, the phalaropes mate, lay eggs, and rear their young. But they do this in ways quite different from most birds.

Instead of the male trying to attract a female, it's the female phalarope that "chases" the male! And when the bigger and more brightly colored female has picked out a male she wants, she won't take no for an answer! She'll bully him by pushing and pecking until he simply gives up. And she will threaten any other female that comes near her mate.

It is the male who makes the nest. He pushes his body into damp, soft ground, making a shallow pit that he lines with grass. The female lays three or four eggs. After that, she generally pays no more attention to her "husband" or her babies. The male phalarope incubates the eggs and does all the work of rearing the young ones after they hatch.

A Frigate Bird (right) attacking a gull in order to steal a fish.

Sky pirate!

A hungry gull, gliding above the ocean, spied movement in the water. Swooping down, it jabbed its bill into the water and caught a small fish. With the fish dangling in its bill, the gull soared upward.

But the gull didn't know that a pirate was following it! The pirate was a very large black bird with extremely long wings and an orange throat. And now, it attacked! It darted at the gull, bumping the smaller bird and jabbing with its bill. The frightened gull dropped its fish.

This was just what the pirate wanted. It dived after the fish, caught it in the air, and swallowed it. The poor gull flew off to look for another meal.

This pirate of the sky is the frigate bird, or man-o'-war bird. A frigate (FRIHG iht) was a fast warship (man-o'-war) of long ago, sometimes used by pirates. The bird got its name because it's such a swift, bold robber!

Frigate birds live along seacoasts in warm parts of the world. Although they are faster

and more powerful fliers than any other sea
bird, they don't usually fly very far out to sea.
They stay near land, snatching up fish and
other sea creatures swimming near the
surface—and robbing gulls, boobies, and other
birds of the fish they have caught.

Male frigate birds have an orange throat. At
mating time, a male's throat swells up until it
looks like a bright red balloon. This helps a
male attract a mate.

The nest of the frigate bird is a platform of
sticks in a small tree or bush. A female frigate
bird lays only one egg. Both she and her mate
feed and take care of the baby. They must
guard it well, for other frigate birds will eat it
if given the chance.

male Frigate Bird

At mating time, a male
Frigate Bird's throat
swells up like a big
red balloon. This helps
the male attract a
mate.

There once was a puffin

Oh, there once was a Puffin
Just the shape of a muffin,
And he lived on an island
In the bright blue sea!

> from *There Once Was a Puffin*
> by Florence Page Jaques

Actually, puffins spend only a few months of each year living on an island. All the rest of the time they live in the northern seas, far from land. Fine swimmers, they use their wings to move through the water. They can also fly, but they spend much more time in the water than in the air. They eat small fishes and other tiny sea creatures that they catch by diving and swimming underwater.

Puffins go to islands only at mating time. Using their bills and feet, pairs of puffins dig a burrow in which the female lays one egg. The parents share the job of incubating the egg. When it hatches, they share the work of feeding the baby with fish—usually two huge meals a day. When the baby is about six weeks old, the parents return to the sea.

At the time the parents leave, the baby is not only too young to fly, but also too heavy! It stays in the burrow, living off its fat, while it grows its flying feathers. After about a week, it leaves the nest and flutters down to the sea. By itself, it learns to swim, fly, and catch fish.

puffin

It's a mystery how a puffin can catch one fish after another without dropping any!

There's a mystery about the way puffins catch fish. A puffin often comes out of the water with five or six slim fish hanging out of its bill. The fish must have been caught one at a time—but how a puffin holds on to one fish when it opens its bill to catch another is a real puzzle!

Black Skimmers feeding

The lower part of a Black Skimmer's bill is longer than the upper part. When the bird is feeding, the long lower bill slices through the water.

Trailblazers

The bird called a Black Skimmer looks as if it has a lower bill that it borrowed from another bird, for the lower bill is much longer than the upper one. Skimmers are the only birds that have such bills. But, of course, there's a good reason for the strange shape of a skimmer's bill. It's a very special tool for getting food.

Black Skimmers live by the sea in parts of North and South America. They eat small fish, shrimp, and other little sea creatures. A hungry Black Skimmer flies close to, or *skims,* the top of the water. It flies with its mouth open, the tip of its long, razor-sharp lower bill slicing through the water. The instant the lower bill touches a fish, the upper bill snaps down. The fish is caught!

The skimmer's way of fishing is also a way of making food come right to it! A skimmer fishes mostly at twilight or dawn, when the water is dark. As it skims along, its lower bill leaves a long, sparkling trail in the water. This attracts fish, which swim up into the trail. So, after flying in one direction for a while, the skimmer turns and skims back along its trail. Any creature that has come up into the trail gets caught!

Because of its bill, a skimmer can't pick up things that are on the ground. But baby skimmers can. Their top and bottom bills are the same length. So, when the parents bring fish and drop them on the ground, the babies can pick them up easily. A young skimmer's lower bill won't get longer until the bird is almost full grown.

Sea gulls

There's really no such thing as a "sea gull."
That's just a name most people use for almost
any kind of gull—Herring Gull, Mew Gull,
Laughing Gull, Ivory Gull, and others.
Because gulls are often seen soaring over
seashores and perched on docks, people think
of them as birds of the sea.

 These birds probably should be called
"shore gulls" instead of "sea gulls"! They are
really shore birds, not sea birds. Most of them

Laughing Gull

Ring-Billed Gull

never fly very far out to sea. And many of them are found far, far from the sea, at lakes and rivers, and even on prairies!

Gulls get their food from both water and land, and they'll eat almost anything. They'll snatch live fish out of the water or eat dead, rotting fish that have drifted onto a beach. They will hang around ships and boats, to feast on food scraps thrown overboard. They'll eat insects, worms, shellfish, berries, seeds, bird eggs, small birds, small animals, and even the flesh of large dead animals such as whales.

Most kinds of gulls are tough, bold, and clever. A Laughing Gull will stand on a pelican's head and steal a fish right out of its big bill! A Herring Gull will steal an egg, or even a baby bird, from the nest of a big

Herring Gulls swarming around a fishing boat
in search of an easy meal.

cormorant. Many kinds of gulls are clever enough to pick up a clam in their bill, fly high, and then drop the clam onto some rocks. This breaks open the shell, so that the bird can feast on the soft meat inside. However, the bird may sometimes have to drop the clam five or six times before the shell breaks open.

Gulls like one another's company. Most of the time they live together in large flocks. At mating time, they gather together by the thousands. The males fight among themselves for the best spots to make a nest. And, after their mates have laid eggs, the males must be on constant guard to defend their young from other gulls that might try to eat the eggs or baby birds!

Gulls that stay near the sea generally make a nest of seaweed and moss. Female gulls lay two or three eggs. These hatch in about twenty days. Baby gulls hatch with open eyes and coats of soft down, or tiny feathers. They can walk in a few hours and run in six or seven days. Their parents feed and protect them for about six weeks, until they can care for themselves.

Gulls are useful creatures. By eating dead things and garbage, they help keep beaches clean. Because they eat many harmful insects, they are a help to farmers. And they are a welcome sight to sailors, because they are a sign that land is near.

Shell-opener

Have you ever seen someone trying to open an oyster shell? It's not easy, unless you have a special tool. And that's just what the bird called an oystercatcher has—its bill is a tool for opening oyster shells!

Oystercatchers live on sandy and stony beaches in many parts of the world. The oysters and other shellfish they eat live on rocks in shallow water near the beach. When the tide goes out, the large clusters of shellfish

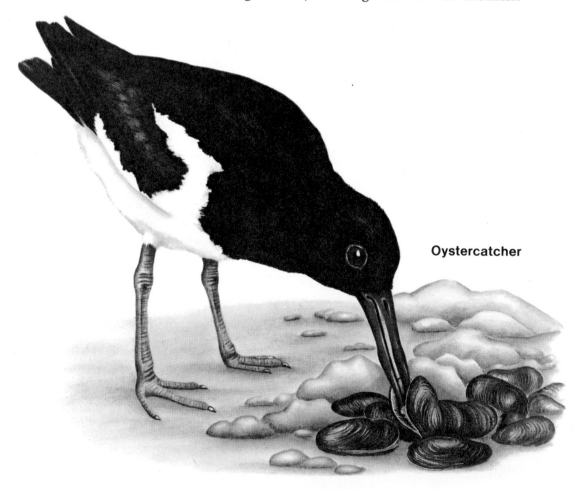

Oystercatcher

are left uncovered. That's when flocks of oystercatchers show up for dinner!

When the oysters are uncovered, they open their shells just a tiny bit. An oystercatcher pokes its thin, flat bill into the tiny crack. It snips the strong muscle that holds the two halves of the shell together. Then, in an instant, it pries the shell apart, and gobbles up the oyster.

Oystercatchers also use their bill to pry limpets and similar creatures off rocks. A limpet is an oysterlike animal, but it has only one shell that covers its back. It creeps over the rocks on its belly. It can grip a rock so firmly that not even a strong man can pull the creature off. But an oystercatcher simply slides its bill between the limpet and the rock. Then it lifts off the limpet, turns it over, and eats it.

Oystercatchers wade in shallow water, plucking up snails and small crabs. They break open the shells by hammering them with their bills. They also push their long bills down into sand to catch worms.

Like many beach-dwelling birds, oystercatchers don't make much of a nest. The female just squats down in the sand and turns around and around many times. This makes a small hollow in which she lays her eggs. Even though the eggs are out in the open, they look so much like pebbles it's almost impossible to find them.

The Stormy Petrel

by Bryan Waller Procter

Up and down!—up and down!
From the base of the wave to the billow's crown,
And amidst the flashing and feathery foam
The stormy petrel finds a home,—
A home, if such a place may be
For her who lives on the wide, wide sea,
On the craggy ice, in the frozen air,
And only seeketh her rocky lair
To warm her young, and to teach them to spring
At once o'er the waves on their stormy wing!

O'er the deep!—o'er the deep!
Where the whale and the shark and the
 swordfish sleep,—
Outflying the blast and the driving rain,
The petrel telleth her tale—in vain;
For the mariner curseth the warning bird
Which bringeth him news of the storm unheard!
Ah! Thus doth the prophet, of good or ill,
Meet hate from the creature he serveth still;
Yet he ne'er falters,—so, petrel, spring
Once more o'er the waves on thy stormy wing!

Storm birds

Sailors once believed that when they saw the birds called storm petrels (PEHT ruhlz), or stormy petrels, a storm was on the way. It is true that flocks of these birds often appear at sea just before a storm.

Storm petrels belong to a large group of birds known as tube-noses. Their nostrils are short tubes on each side of their upper bill. These tubes take salt out of the birds' bodies. These birds drink salty seawater, and the salt would stay in their bodies if they could not get rid of it this way.

There are actually about nineteen different kinds of storm petrels, but they all live the same way. They spend most of their life far out over the ocean, hundreds of miles (kilometers) from land. When they must rest, they just glide down to the water and ride the waves, floating like corks.

Storm petrels feed on tiny sea creatures that they pluck from the water with their bills. When some kinds of storm petrels feed, they seem to be walking on the water, with their feet touching the sea.

The only time storm petrels come to land is during the mating season. They make their nests under stones, or dig tunnels in the ground with their bills. A mother petrel lays one egg. She and her mate take turns incubating it until it hatches.

Wandering Albatrosses

These birds spend most of their lives flying over the sea. They come to land only once a year, to mate and raise a family.

Gooney bird

There's a sea bird that has many strange names. For hundreds of years, sailors have thought these birds stupid and called them "gooney birds." Japanese fishermen know them as *bakadori,* or "fool-birds." And to the Dutch, this bird is a *mallemok,* or "stupid gull."

On land, or on the deck of a ship, this bird seems stupid and often looks very silly. It walks with a funny, awkward waddle. To take off from level ground, it runs along even more awkwardly, flapping its wings frantically. As often as not, it crashes before it can get into the air. And when it comes in for a landing, it is very likely to go sprawling across the sand!

But in the air, a "gooney bird" is no longer clumsy. It is a graceful, beautiful flier, and can soar for hours without flapping its wings.

This bird's real name is albatross (AL buh traws). It is related to the petrels, for it, too, is a tube-nose. But while petrels are the smallest of all sea birds, albatrosses are the biggest. The wings of a Wandering Albatross measure as much as eleven and a half feet (3.5 meters) from tip to tip.

The way of life of an albatross is like that of a petrel, except that an albatross soars and glides while a petrel must flutter and flap its wings to stay in the air. Albatrosses soar over the sea for months at a time. They will follow a ship for days, hardly ever coming to rest on the water. They feed on scraps of food thrown from ships, or on fish and squid. The only time they come to land is to mate.

Albatrosses have long been part of the lore and legend of the sea. To superstitious sailors, they were the spirits of men lost overboard in storms. The appearance of an albatross was also a sign of wind or fog. And to kill an albatross brought bad luck.

Long ago, sailors believed that killing an albatross brought bad luck. The poem, "The Rime of the Ancient Mariner," by Samuel Taylor Coleridge, tells of the bad luck that befell a ship when one of the crew killed an albatross. As punishment, the bird's body was hung from the sailor's neck. The saying, "to have an albatross about one's neck," means to have a great trouble to bear.

Fish hawk

Some distance from a rocky coastline, a bird soared in great circles over the sea. It was a keen-eyed bird of prey, with hooked beak and sharp talons—an osprey (AHS pree), also called a fish hawk.

The bird circled slowly, peering down into the gray-green water. Then, abruptly, it dived. With its sharp-clawed feet stretched out in front of it, it plunged into the sea. Moments later it was in the air, a large fish dangling from its claws.

Ospreys live along seacoasts throughout most of the world. Some also live near lakes and rivers. These birds eat mostly fish and live where fish are plentiful.

Fish are slippery creatures, hard to grab and hang onto. But an osprey's foot is a marvelous fish-catching tool. Its talons can grip with tremendous strength. And the bottom of each foot is covered with rough, spiky scales that act like little hooks. A fish simply *can't* slip out of an osprey's clutches.

At mating time, ospreys build nests that are tremendous piles of such stuff as seaweed and dried branches. Ospreys usually choose trees for nesting places, but they will also make nests at the very top of telephone poles.

The male osprey takes care of feeding his mate and babies. He brings fish to them, which he tears into small pieces. He gives the

An osprey feeding
its chicks.

female one piece at a time. She eats some
pieces and tears others into smaller bits,
which she gives to the babies. Unlike most
baby birds, which are wild and noisy at
feeding time, baby ospreys are quiet and
usually have "good manners."

Royal Penguins

These are one of a few kinds of penguins that have crests of feathers on their heads.

Penguins

Do you think of penguins as fat, funny little birds that are always sliding and waddling about on the snow and ice of Antarctica? Well, the fact is that penguins spend most of their lives in the water! They are really creatures of the sea rather than the land. They go onto land only to mate, lay eggs, and rear their young.

Penguins do waddle comically when they walk on land. But they are swift and graceful in water—the finest swimmers of all birds. They can't fly at all in the air, but they use their wings, which are really flippers, to "fly" through the water. They swim and dive

Royal Penguins and King Penguins on the way to their rookery, or mating place.

swiftly after the small fish, squid, and tiny crablike creatures they eat.

Although the sea is their home, penguins are in constant danger when they are in the water. The Antarctic Ocean is also the home of fast, sharp-toothed leopard seals, which prey on penguins. Big, swift killer whales are also a danger.

All penguins live in the southern half of the world. There are eighteen different kinds of them. Penguins of each kind generally stay together in large groups. At mating time, most kinds gather by the thousands, and even by the millions, at their mating places. Each kind of penguin has its own mating place. Some go to Antarctica, and some to rocky islands nearby. Others go to grassy or sandy places on the coasts of South America, South Africa, or Australia.

The biggest of all penguins, the Emperor Penguins, go to Antarctica. In the autumn, they swim to the great beaches of ice that form there, and gather in huge groups. In long lines, they march for miles (kilometers) to their age-old mating place. They spend the next two months picking out mates.

By the time the female Emperor Penguins begin to lay eggs, it's the middle of winter.

Emperor Penguins

These penguins stand about four feet (120 centimeters) tall. They are the largest of all penguins.

This is a time of complete darkness in Antarctica—for two months, the sun never rises. The temperature is often as low as seventy degrees below zero, Fahrenheit (−57° Celsius). But the penguins huddle together for warmth. Their feathers and the fat under their skin also keep them warm.

On the Antarctic ice there is nothing with which to make a nest. So, Emperor Penguins don't have nests. The female simply lays her one egg on the ice. At once, her mate scoops it up onto the top of his feet. Then he hunches over so that his belly covers the egg to keep it warm.

After the females lay their eggs, they leave the mating place and go back to the sea. The job of incubating the eggs is done by the males. They now stand, hardly moving, for as much as *two months,* keeping the eggs warm. During all that time, they never eat! They live off the fat stored in their bodies.

So, a baby Emperor Penguin is hatched by its father. And it gets its first meal from its father. A male Emperor Penguin makes a nourishing, soupy liquid in its throat, for the baby to eat.

The babies all hatch at about the same time. Soon after, their mothers begin returning. As the mothers make their way through the huge crowd of males and babies, they call out. Each male recognizes his mate's voice, and answers. The females recognize the

Adélie Penguins
diving into the
Antarctic Ocean.

males' voices, and make their way to them
and the babies.

The females are now fat and healthy. They
take over the job of caring for the babies. The
males, very thin and hungry by now, head for
the sea. There they gorge on fish and shrimp
until they gain back the weight they lost.

The penguins called Adélie (uh DAY lee)
Penguins also go to Antarctica for their
mating season. But Adélies lay their eggs in

the springtime. They go to places where the snow has melted, and where there are stones lying about on the muddy ground. They pile up stones to make nests. However, there are never quite enough stones to go around—so the Adélies often steal stones from one another's nests!

The Magellan (muh JEHL uhn) Penguins rear their young on a sandy beach on the southern coast of South America. They dig shallow burrows in the sand in which they lay their eggs. The Royal Penguins go to a green island between Antarctica and Australia, and lay their eggs in a small, muddy valley. The Little Blue Penguins nest in holes or under rocks on islands near Australia and New Zealand. These birds, the smallest of penguins, are about one foot (30 centimeters) high.

A Magellan Penguin incubating an egg.

Other birds of the sea and shore

Great Skua and Northern Gannet

A Great Skua (right) trying to make a Northern Gannet give up a fish. Great Skuas are found in areas around the Arctic, North Atlantic, and Antarctic oceans. Northern Gannets live in areas around the North Atlantic Ocean.

Caspian Tern

(North America, Europe, Asia, Africa, Australia, New Zealand)

Double-Crested Cormorant

(western North Atlantic Ocean)

Blue-Footed Booby

(tropical eastern Pacific Ocean)

Birds of the
Far North

At home on the tundra

Spring has come to the tundra—that vast, icy plain that lies in the Far North. The ice covering the soil melts, giving seeds a chance to sprout. Grass and flowers shoot up. The willow and alder trees, no bigger than bushes, are shaggy with new leaves.

In a clump of grass, a bird crouches, motionless. It is fairly large, with black, brown, and white feathers—a female Willow Ptarmigan (TAHR muh guhn) sitting on her eggs. Her nest is just a little hollow she has scraped out of the dirt and lined with grass.

photographs on pages 260–261

Willow Ptarmigans: on the tundra in spring and in summer feathers

A shadow slides over the ptarmigan's body. It is a gull, circling overhead. The gull drops lower, eyeing the bird on her nest. If the gull can frighten her into leaving, it can steal an egg or two to eat.

The ptarmigan sees the gull and senses what it is up to. But she doesn't move. She merely gives a cry—a signal!

At once, a brown and white body shoots up from an alder tree not far away. It is the female's mate. He whirs straight for the gull and smashes into it, knocking it to the ground! Then he sails back to his hiding place, to continue his watch over his family.

A male Willow Ptarmigan is a fighter! He will fight fiercely to protect his mate and her eggs. In fact, he has to be able to fight to get a mate.

In early spring, a male ptarmigan picks out a territory. He struts about, making cackling sounds—*karr-ack-ack-ack*! If another male appears, the owner of the territory cackles a loud war cry that sounds like, "go back, go back," or, "tobacco, tobacco"! Usually there's a fight that ends only when one bird runs away. Only the strongest males can keep a territory and win a mate.

After baby ptarmigans hatch, both parents care for them and defend them until they can fly. During spring and summer the birds wander about, feasting on insects, seeds, and leaves. Toward the end of summer, there are many fruits and berries for them to eat. But spring and summer last for only two months on the tundra. Then snow begins to fall. It will cover the plain for some ten months!

Many birds and other creatures leave the tundra before this happens. But not the Willow Ptarmigans. They are fitted for life in a cold, snowy land.

Walking in snow day after day is impossible for most birds. Their feet would freeze. But short feathers keep a Willow Ptarmigan's feet warm. The feathers also act like snowshoes. They make it possible for the bird to walk on the snow without sinking in.

For most birds, living in a treeless, snow-covered land would be terribly dangerous. Their colors would enable hungry

A Willow Ptarmigan's feet are covered with feathers. This keeps them warm and also helps the bird walk on snow more easily.

enemies to see them easily. But in winter, ptarmigans turn snow-white except for a bit of the tail. This makes the ptarmigans almost invisible against the snow, so that enemies such as an Arctic fox or a Snowy Owl can't see them very well.

Living on a flat, snow-covered plain with no place to roost is no problem for a ptarmigan. When one of these birds wants to sleep, it just burrows into the snow. The bird's own body heat keeps this little "igloo" warm. As for food during winter, a ptarmigan lives on buds that grow on the branches of the little willow and alder trees.

Willow Ptarmigans are true citizens of the Far North. They're tough, hardy birds, well able to survive in a cold, snowy world.

The Snowy Owl

The tundra is the home of the chubby white and brown owl known as the Snowy Owl. In spring, when the tundra blooms, Snowy Owls mate. But in this barren land, life is far from easy for the baby owls. Many of them don't survive. If their father can't bring enough food, some starve to death. Others become food for prowling foxes and weasels. If an icy rain falls, some may die from cold.

Even the young owls that grow up and leave the nest aren't out of danger. They have only a short time to learn to hunt before the harsh northern winter begins. If they don't learn soon enough, they will die.

Snowy Owls hunt mostly lemmings—little plump, furry creatures that look like mice. But these owls also go after rabbits, ducks, ptarmigans, and almost any other creature they can manage to kill. During summer in the Far North, the sun never sets for weeks at a time. So, a Snowy Owl does its hunting in daylight.

When winter begins, some of the owls stay where they are, while others move a little way south. Now the hunting is harder, for in winter the little lemmings keep to their underground burrows. The owls take what they can—even fish. During winter in the Far North, the sun does not rise for weeks on end, so the owls hunt in darkness.

Snowy Owl

This owl has killed a lemming. These small, mouselike animals are a Snowy Owl's main prey.

    Every few years, when food is very scarce, the Snowy Owls must move much farther south. Then, people in Sweden, Norway, Canada, and parts of the United States have a chance to see these white owls of the Far North.

Odin's messengers

The Norse god Odin was said to have two magical pet Ravens that were his spies and messengers.

Long ago, the people of Scandinavia and other northern lands believed that Ravens were the messengers of Odin, the greatest of the Norse gods. Odin was said to keep two Ravens that he sent out into the world each morning. In the evening, they returned and told him all they had seen.

The Norse people thought that Ravens were smart birds. And so they are. They can be taught to count up to three or four and to say a few words. Sometimes, Ravens will team up to do a job—for example, to steal food from an Eskimo dog. One bird will get the dog's attention by pecking it on the tail. When the angry dog turns to chase the bird away, the other Raven darts in and grabs the food!

Ravens are also very bold and playful. They are brave enough to attack and drive off large falcons and other birds of prey. They play "games" by passing sticks and stones back and forth and teasing each other with them. And they seem to enjoy doing aerial acrobatics.

Ravens generally live in pairs or in little groups. They take good care of their young. A mother Raven even gives her babies baths! She dunks herself in water and then rubs the babies with her wet feathers.

When it comes to food, Ravens will eat just about anything. In spring and summer, they steal the eggs of eagles and snatch up baby gulls. And they'll gladly feast on people's garbage. But what these birds mostly eat is the flesh of dead animals.

The largest members of the crow family, Ravens can live almost anywhere. They are found on mountains, plains, and deserts throughout the northern half of the world. But a great many Ravens live all year round on the icy tundra of the Far North.

A Raven sitting by its nest and young.

Masters of the northern sky

Streaking over the tundra, close to the ground, speeds a large bird. Its big eyes and hooked beak mark it as a bird of prey. It is a Gyrfalcon (JUR fawl kuhn), the largest of the swift hunting birds called falcons.

The Gyrfalcon skims up and over a rise in the ground. On the other side of the rise sits a white-feathered ptarmigan. Startled by the sudden sight of the Gyrfalcon rushing toward it, the ptarmigan rises into the air. But in an instant, the Gyrfalcon smashes into it. The ptarmigan tumbles lifeless to the ground.

Gyrfalcons live and hunt all year round on the tundra. They are swift, powerful birds—masters of the northern sky. During the long tundra winter, they hunt mostly Willow Ptarmigans. In the spring and summer, they go after lemmings, rabbits, and many

kinds of birds. By flying close to the ground, they can often take their prey by surprise.

Gyrfalcons nest on cliffs near the coast or along river valleys. The nest is a pile of sticks, bones, wads of animal skin, fur, and feathers. The female lays her eggs before the tundra spring begins.

The babies hatch about the time ptarmigans and other birds are beginning to lay their eggs. Thus, young Gyrfalcons are learning to fly when other baby birds of the tundra are hatching. Young Gyrfalcons learn how to hunt by going after baby ptarmigans that are just beginning to waddle about.

People have enjoyed falconry—the sport of hunting with trained falcons—for about four thousand years. The falcons are taught to bring back the birds they catch. During the Middle Ages, the most prized hunting falcon of all, which only a king could own, was the Gyrfalcon of the Far North!

Snowbirds

Snow Buntings spend the spring and summer
in rocky parts of the Arctic. Like many other
birds, they fly south for the winter. But for
Snow Buntings, "south" is still in the cold

Snow Buntings

northern parts of the world, where the snow lies thick upon the ground.

Snow Buntings seem to like snow and bitter cold. Chirping cheerfully, they are at home on snow-covered ground. At night, they don't roost in trees—they just go to sleep on the snow, protected only by weeds or brush. As for food, they eat the seeds on the tops of dried grass and weeds that stick up out of snowdrifts.

Snow Buntings don't stay in the "south" very long. As soon as the snow melts a bit, foretelling the coming of spring, the buntings gather in large flocks. They head back to their mating places. Some Snow Buntings go farther north to mate and rear their young than any other kind of land bird.

When the flocks arrive, the males go off by themselves to pick a territory. In time, nearly every male is joined by a female.

The female uses moss, feathers, and bits of animal fur to make a nest under rocks or in cracks in the ground. Just when insects are becoming numerous in the Far North, the baby birds hatch. The mother and father buntings feed their babies mosquitoes, moths, spiders, and other tiny creatures.

By fall, the young birds are able to fly. That's when the buntings start to gather into flocks again. Soon, they are flying "south"—to where people are shivering in the snowy cold that Snow Buntings love!

Other birds
of the Far North

shawk and its young

Ross's Gull

Purple Sandpiper

Birds and You

Bird watching

Would you like to be an unofficial scientist?
You can be!

Throughout the world there are millions of
people who are "bird watchers." They're
actually unofficial scientists. They study birds,
just as scientists do, to learn about the birds'
ways of life. They keep notes on the things
they see. Many of them soon become true
"bird experts."

You can easily become a bird watcher and
unofficial scientist, too. No matter where you
live, there are sure to be birds for you to
observe in summer and winter.

If you have a backyard, you'll be surprised
at how many different kinds of birds visit it.

**photographs
on pages 276–277**

bird watchers on the
coast of Scotland, and
a boy and his pet canary

And if you put a bird feeder outside a window, you'll have a chance to see many birds close up. A birdbath is another good way to attract birds. If you live near a woods, lake, meadow, or park, you can look for birds in those places.

When you first begin bird watching, just try to see how many different kinds of birds you can find. You may want to carry a notebook and pencil so that you can write down a description of each bird. Try to describe the bird's size and shape. Is it a large bird like a crow, or a very small one like a sparrow? Is it round and plump, or is its body long and slim? Are its legs long or short? Are its wings rounded or pointed? Most important of all, is its bill long and thin, or short and fat, or is it hooked at the tip?

How is the bird colored? Does it have bright patches of color anywhere on its body? Does it have spots or bars on its wings, or a stripe over its eyes, or a patch that looks like a bib at its throat?

Notice how the bird stands and moves. Is it perched in a tree or standing on the ground? Is its body upright, or sort of stretched out in a line? Does it stand very still, or does it often flick its tail or wings? Does it move one foot after another when it walks or runs, or does it hop with both feet? Does it fly often, or stand still? Write such things down.

Of course, you'll want to know the names of the birds you see. Many bird watchers carry books with pictures of hundreds of birds in them. Such books are called field guides. A field guide can help you find out the name of each kind of bird. You will find field guides in your public library and at most bookstores. Field guides are also full of interesting facts about the birds you see.

You'll soon recognize birds after you've seen them more than once. Each time you spot a certain kind, see if you can notice something new about it. You'll be surprised at how many kinds of birds you will see. Many bird watchers keep lists of the birds they have seen

each month, each year, or throughout their lives!

Binoculars are a big help when you are bird watching. With binoculars you can see birds clearly from a distance. You won't have to get so close that you frighten the birds away.

You can, however, enjoy bird watching even without a field guide or binoculars. Just go where the birds are and watch what they do. Seashores, lakesides, marshes, ponds, and golf courses are good places to find birds that are easy to watch. You'll find that it's a lot of fun to watch birds go about their ways of life!

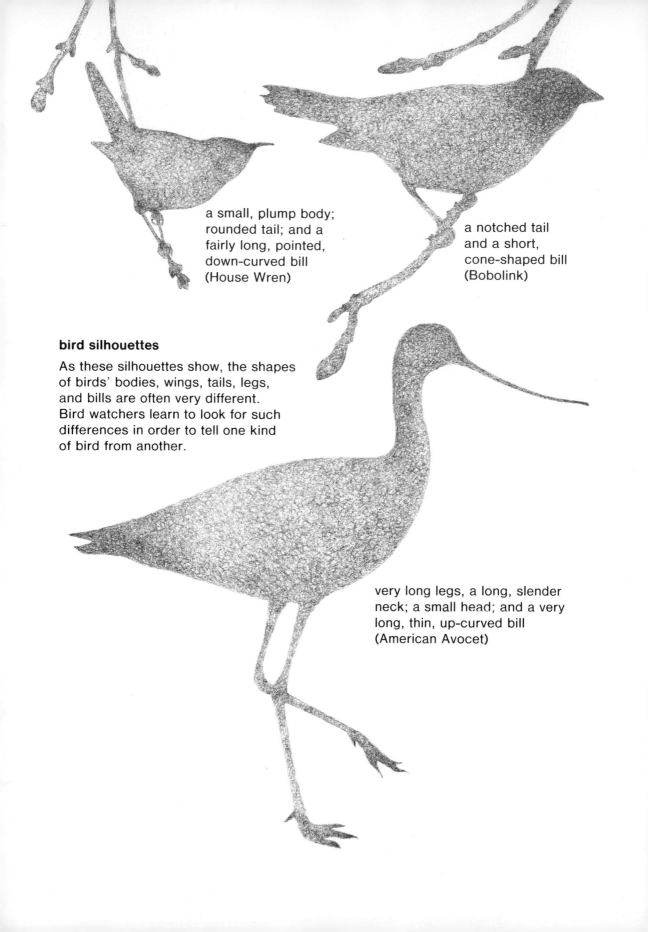

a small, plump body; rounded tail; and a fairly long, pointed, down-curved bill (House Wren)

a notched tail and a short, cone-shaped bill (Bobolink)

bird silhouettes

As these silhouettes show, the shapes of birds' bodies, wings, tails, legs, and bills are often very different. Bird watchers learn to look for such differences in order to tell one kind of bird from another.

very long legs, a long, slender neck; a small head; and a very long, thin, up-curved bill (American Avocet)

a long, cone-shaped
bill and rounded tail
(Red-Winged Blackbird)

a very short, pointed
bill; forked tail; and
long, pointed wings
(Barn Swallow)

a very short, hooked bill;
rounded wings; and square tail
(Whippoorwill)

a long, rounded
bill and long legs
(Lesser Golden Plover)

Build a birdhouse

You can attract some kinds of birds to your backyard by putting a birdhouse there. Many of the birds that live in towns and cities will gladly nest in birdhouses. You should put up a birdhouse in early spring, before most birds return from their wintering grounds to choose their summer homes. This way you'll have a better chance of attracting one to your birdhouse.

Here is a way to make a birdhouse out of an empty one-quart (0.95-liter) milk carton. You'll need a spray can of black flat enamel paint, some wire, and some tape. You may need a grown-up to help you make the birdhouse and to put it up. Don't be afraid to ask for help.

First, open the top of the milk carton, where the pouring spout is. Open it all the way. Wash out the carton and let it dry.

Next, with your spray can of black paint, paint the inside of the carton. Do this outdoors on old newspapers. The black paint will make the birdhouse dark. Birds like dark places for their nests.

Now, make two pairs of holes on one side of the carton, as shown in the picture. Each hole should be just big enough for the wire to fit through. One pair of holes should be about two inches (5 centimeters) from the top of the side. The other pair should be about two

inches from the bottom. The two holes in each pair should be about two inches (5 cm) apart.

You should also punch one or two tiny holes in the bottom of the carton. This is to let out water, in case rain should ever get into the birdhouse.

Near the top of the side that is *opposite* the two pairs of holes, cut a round hole no more than $1\frac{1}{4}$ inches (3 cm) wide. This is just the

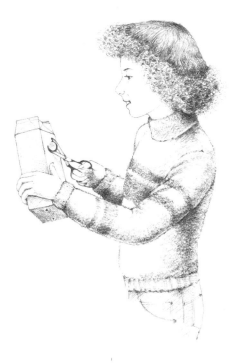

right size for sparrows and other small birds. It's easy to make this hole with sharp scissors, but be careful. Push one point of the scissors in to get started, and then cut out a circle. This hole will be the doorway. It doesn't matter if it isn't perfectly round.

Pick out the tree where you want to put the
birdhouse. You will need two pieces of wire.
Each piece has to be long enough to go
around the tree trunk, with about eight inches
(20 cm) left over. Slide one piece of wire
through the top pair of holes in the side of
your carton—in one hole and out the other.
Slide the other piece through the bottom pair
of holes.

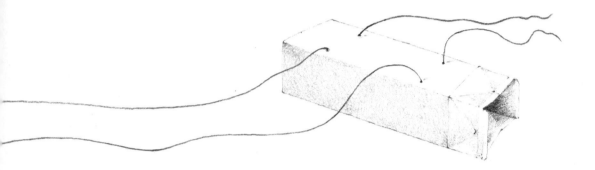

Fold the top of the carton together again,
and fasten it tightly with tape. If you have a
stapler, staple the top of the carton together
for extra strength.

You may want to paint the outside of the carton to make it look nice and last longer. You can use exterior latex flat enamel. If your birdhouse will be in the shade, use green or brown paint. If it will be in the sun, white paint will keep the house cool.

When the paint is dry and the smell is gone, your birdhouse is ready to put on the tree. A grown-up may have to do this for you because the house should be at least eight feet (2.4 meters) from the ground. Each piece of wire must be wound tightly around the tree trunk, and the ends must be twisted tightly together. The house must be secure, so it won't fall.

If you want a house for bigger birds, such as bluebirds, use a larger milk carton. Make your door-hole about $1\frac{1}{2}$ inches (3.8 cm) wide, but no wider. If it is too big, starlings may take over the birdhouse and drive out any birds that are already there! ·

Canaries and other flying birds should have enough room in the cage to fly.

Birds as pets

Do birds make good pets? Some birds do. Many people keep canaries, finches, parakeets, or parrots in their home.

Most of these birds are raised in cages and sold in pet shops. They have never lived in the wild. But in many ways, they are not very different from their wild relatives! To be happy and healthy, pet birds need many of the same things wild birds need.

Wild birds hop, climb, and fly. Pet birds need exercise, too. If you plan to get a pet bird, you should get a cage that is big enough to allow the bird to use its feet and wings. Your bird will get even more exercise if you let it fly freely in a room for part of each day—but make sure that all the windows and doors are closed. Otherwise, your pet may fly away!

Wild birds eat many kinds of food. A pet bird needs fresh food every day—several kinds of seeds, and also fresh, clean greenery. "Salad" for birds can be almost any green vegetable people eat: lettuce, turnip greens, and other leafy things. Parrots like some kinds of fruit, too. And, of course, all birds need fresh water to drink.

Be sure your pet bird has a daily supply of fresh drinking water.

Wild birds keep themselves clean. Pet birds want to keep clean, too. If you put a special "bathtub" of water in its cage, a parakeet or canary will bathe on its own. But, of course, a pet bird can't sweep and scrub to keep its cage clean. That's the owner's job, and it should be done often!

Wild birds are busy. They spend a lot of time feeding and caring for themselves and their young. A pet bird needs things to do, too. Otherwise, it will become bored and lonely.

With patience, you can teach a pet bird to sit on your finger or shoulder. And many parakeets and parrots can be trained to talk. Parakeets like to push and pull small bird toys. Parrots enjoy using their beaks and feet to climb and to hold things. And all of these birds enjoy being in a room where people come and go, rather than in a room by themselves.

Pet birds do many of the same things wild birds do. You can expect your pet to molt its old feathers and grow new ones, just as it would in the wild. And a pair of birds will want to nest and to feed and raise their young. At times like these, pet birds need special care.

Should you get a bird for a pet? If you are trying to decide, you can find many good books that will tell you more about birds and bird care. You can also visit birds in pet shops

A mirror in the cage helps keep some kinds of birds from becoming lonely.

and talk to people who own birds. A veterinarian can answer some of your questions, too. Then, if you really want a bird, you will be able to decide which kind of bird is best for you. And you will know how to raise a happy, healthy pet.

Books to Read

If you like birds and want to find out more about them, there are lots of good books you will enjoy. A few of them are listed here. Your school or public library will have many others.

Ages 5 to 8

Baltimore Orioles by Barbara Brenner (Harper & Row, 1974)
The family life of a fascinating songbird is simply and accurately described in a book that beginning readers will enjoy.

The Barn Owl by Phyllis Flower (Harper & Row, 1978)
The drawings in this picture book show how the owls nest, how baby owls are cared for, and what happens when it is time for the babies to leave home.

Birds Are Flying by John Kaufmann (Crowell, 1979)
Different birds fly in different ways. Here are examples of fast, slow, and fancy flying—and an explanation of why some birds can't fly at all.

Bird Talk by Roma Gans (Crowell, 1971)
The author tells how and when birds make different kinds of sounds.

Bird Watchers and Bird Feeders by Glenn O. Blough (McGraw-Hill, 1963)
Here are easy ways to recognize common birds and hints for what and how to feed them.

Brave Little Hummingbird by Virginia Frances Voight (Putnam, 1971)
A tiny Ruby-Throated Hummingbird, less than four inches (10 centimeters) in length, makes a long journey from Central America to New England.

The Chicken and the Egg by Oxford Scientific Films (Putnam, 1979)
Photographs show how chickens live, grow, and find their place, or pecking order, in the flock.

C'mon Ducks! by Kay Cooper (Messner, 1978)
Two young girls raise four Muscovy ducklings and record their growth.

Ducks Don't Get Wet by Augusta Golden (Crowell, 1965)
A simple experiment shows young readers why ducks shed water.

A First Look at Birds by Millicent E. Selsam and Joyce Hunt (Walker, 1973)
Basic questions about birds and the ways they adapt to different environments are answered in this book.

Five Nests by Carolyn Arnold (Dutton, 1980)
Stories of five bird families show some of the many ways different birds care for their young.

The Hungry Snowbird by Richard Farrar (Coward, 1975)
Unlike birds that fly to warmer places, juncos migrate and feed in cold climates.

Penguin's Way by Johanna Johnston (Doubleday, 1962)
This picture book gives a close-up view of the impressive Emperor penguin.

When Birds Change Their Feathers by Roma Gans (Crowell, 1980)
Why do birds molt? This book gives a simple answer and tell how different birds change old feathers for new ones.

Wild Turkeys by Julian May (Holiday, 1973)
Wild turkeys, relatives of the Thanksgiving bird, fight for survival.

Ages 9 to 12

Birds in the Street: The City Pigeon Book by Winifred and Cecil Lubell (Parents, 1971)
This history of pigeons tells how the birds have adapted to city life—and how people have adapted to them.

Birds That Stopped Flying by Elizabeth S. Austin (Random House, 1969)
Some birds have adapted to life on the ground and can survive without flying.

The Bird's Woodland: What Lives There by Richard Farrar (Coward, 1976)
Story and pictures show how woodlands provide homes and food for birds.

Bluebird Rescue by Joan Rattner Heilman (Lothrop, 1982)
The author tells why the bluebird population is shrinking and what can be done to bring bluebirds back.

Falcon Flight by Ida and Frank Graham (Delacorte, 1978)
Peregrine falcons have nearly disappeared. Here is a story of their life in the wild and the efforts to save them.

Fly Away Free by Joan Hewett (Walker, 1981)
A young veterinarian rescues an injured pelican and nurses it back to health.

The Gulls of Smuttynose Island by Jack Denton Scott (Putnam, 1977)
Rocky New England islands are the summer home for thousands of gulls—birds with an unusual social life.

An Introduction to Birds by John Kieran (Doubleday, 1965)
Here is an informal guide that will help beginning bird watchers.

Nature's Nursery: Baby Birds by Robert G. Hudson (John Day, 1971)
Photos show how fourteen kinds of baby birds are fed and cared for. The book also explains imprinting in baby birds.

Owls: Hunters of the Night by Margaret Wheeler Sadoway (Lerner, 1981)
Here are some interesting facts about owls, together with descriptions of eighteen kinds found in North America.

Penguins by Bernard Stonehouse (McGraw-Hill, 1979)
Penguins are especially suited to life at sea. This book describes many kinds and tells how they live.

Have You Ever Heard of a Kangaroo Bird? by Barbara Brenner (Coward, 1980)
Short chapters tell about the kangaroo bird, the bower bird, and other birds that live and behave in amazing ways.

Puffins, Come Back! by Judy Friedman (Dodd, 1981)
Scientists have tried to start a new colony of puffins on a rocky island where the birds once lived.

Roadrunners and Other Cuckoos by Aline Amon (Atheneum, 1978)
Roadrunners can fly—but they walk instead. This book explains their behavior and the unusual behavior of other members of the cuckoo family.

The Submarine Bird by Jack Denton Scott (Putnam, 1980)
The "submarines" are cormorants—masterful diving and fishing birds.

Vultures by Ann W. Turner (McKay, 1973)
The life of these scavenger birds is explored in a book that includes many related species.

New Words

Here are some of the words you have
met in this book. Several of them may
be new to you. All are useful to know,
and many have something to do with
birds. Next to each word, you'll see how
to say the word: **abound** (uh BOWND).
The part in capital letters is said more
loudly than the rest of the word. One or
two sentences under each word tell what
the word means.

abound (uh BOWND)
Abound means to have plenty of or to
be plentiful.

alight (uh LYT)
Alight means to fly down and land.

brood (brood)
To brood means to keep a baby bird
warm and safe. A bird broods its
babies by crouching over them and
protecting them with its wings.

burrow (BUR oh)
A burrow is a hole an animal digs for
a home or a hiding place.

Celsius (SEHL see uhs)
Celsius is the name of a scale for
measuring temperature. It is part of
the metric system of measurement.
On the Celsius scale, water freezes at
0 degrees and boils at 100 degrees. *See
also* Fahrenheit. (For more
information, see Volume 7, *How
Things Work,* pages 138–139.)

colony (KAHL uh nee)
A colony is many animals or plants,
all of the same kind, that live or grow
in one place.

dense (dehns)
Dense means thick or packed closely.
In a dense forest, the trees grow very
close together.

desolate (DEHS uh liht)
Desolate means empty and not lived
in. A desolate land is a place in which
very few plants or animals can live
and grow.

devote (dih VOHT)
Devote means to give time or
attention to a person or thing. Parents
devote themselves to their children.

down (down)
Down is fine, soft feathers. Some baby
birds are covered with down when
they hatch.

extinct (ehk STIHNGKT)
Extinct means no longer living. Any
kind of plant or animal that no longer
lives on the earth is extinct. (For
more information, see Volume 5,
About Animals, pages 294–303.)

Fahrenheit (FAR uhn hyt)
Fahrenheit is the name of a scale for
measuring temperature. On the
Fahrenheit scale, water freezes at 32
degrees and boils at 212 degrees. *See
also* Celsius. (For more information,
see Volume 7, *How Things Work,*
pages 138–139.)

gorge (gawrj)
Gorge means to eat until full; to stuff
with food.

gouge (gowj)
Gouge means to dig out.

incubate (IHN kyuh bayt)
Incubate means to keep eggs warm so
they can hatch. Most birds incubate
their eggs by sitting on them.

incubation (ihn kyuh BAY shuhn)
Incubation is keeping eggs warm. One
or both of the parent birds care for
the eggs during incubation.

incubator (IHN kyuh bay tuhr)
An incubator is a covered box or
other shelter used to keep eggs warm,
as a parent bird would.

instinct (IHN stihngkt)
An instinct is a natural way of doing
something, without being taught how
to do it. Animals are born with
instincts that make them do certain
things or behave in certain ways.
Birds build nests by instinct, without
learning from other birds.

microscopic (my kruh SKAHP ihk)
Something that is microscopic is so

small that it can only be seen through a microscope. It can't be seen with the eyes alone.

migrate (MY grayt)
Migrate means to move from one living place to another. Some kinds of birds, insects, and other animals migrate. (For more information, see Volume 5, *About Animals,* pages 180–181.)

migration (my GRAY shuhn)
A migration is the trip animals make when they migrate, or change homes. Bird migrations often take place when seasons change.

molt (mohlt)
Molt means to shed old feathers, skin, hair, shell, antlers, or other things that grow on the body to make room for new growth. When birds molt, they lose their old feathers and grow new ones. Insects, spiders, snakes, and many other creatures shed their entire outer skin when they molt.

nourish (NUR ihsh)
Nourish means to make something grow or keep something healthy with food. Nourishing foods are foods that are good for keeping living creatures healthy.

order (AWR duhr)
An order is a group of plants or animals that are alike in some way or ways, but are also different from one another in certain ways. Many kinds of plants or animals may belong to a single order. Crows and birds of paradise belong to the same order (perching birds), even though they don't look at all alike.

perch (purch)
Perch means to rest on a branch, wire, or similar thing above the ground. Many birds perch in trees and bushes.

perish (PEHR ihsh)
Perish means to die.

preen (preen)
Preen means to smooth the feathers with the beak. Preening is a bird's way of cleaning itself.

propel (pruh PEHL)
Propel means to drive or push something forward.

quill (kwihl)
A quill is a large, strong feather with a hollow stem that grows on the wing or tail of a bird.

rear (rihr)
Rear means to take care of young ones while they are growing up.

roost (roost)
Roost means to perch somewhere to rest or to sleep.

scrawny (SKRAW nee)
Scrawny means thin or skinny.

soar (sawr)
Soar means to fly with the help of the wind or rising air. A bird soars by stretching out its wings and letting the wind carry it along.

spry (spry)
Spry means lively and active.

taper (TAY puhr)
Taper means to become gradually smaller toward one end.

territory (TEHR uh tawr ee)
A territory is an area an animal chooses for a place to live. A male bird guards its territory and will not let other male birds of the same kind live there. (For more information, see Volume 5, *About Animals,* pages 224–225.)

transparent (trans PAIR uhnt)
A transparent material lets light through so that things on the other side can be seen clearly. Clear glass is transparent.

veterinarian
(veht uhr uh NAIR ee uhn)
A veterinarian is a doctor who treats animals.

waterlogged (WAWT uhr lawgd)
Waterlogged means soaked through with water. Something that is waterlogged is so heavy that it will hardly float.

Illustration Acknowledgments

The publishers of *Childcraft* gratefully acknowledge the courtesy of the following photographers, agencies, and organizations for illustrations in this volume. When all the illustrations for a sequence of pages are from a single source, the inclusive page numbers are given. Credits should be read from left to right, top to bottom, on their respective pages. All illustrations are the exclusive property of the publishers of *Childcraft* unless names are marked with an asterisk (*).

Cover: Aristocrat and Standard Binding—© Rod Planck, Tom Stack & Associates*
Heritage Binding—Patricia Wynne; © Leonard Lee Rue III, Tom Stack & Associates*; Yoshi Miyake; © Gunter Zeisler, Bruce Coleman Ltd.*; © Rod Planck, Tom Stack & Associates*; © Michael Gore, Nature Photographers Ltd.*; © H. Rivarola, Bruce Coleman Ltd.*; Patricia Wynne; © Bruce M. Wellman, Tom Stack & Associates*

1: © Gordon Langsbury, Bruce Coleman Ltd.*
2–3: © L.C. Marigo, Bruce Coleman Ltd.*
8–9: © L.R. Dawson, Bruce Coleman Ltd.*; © Christopher Crowley, Tom Stack & Associates*
10–11: © Anthony Mercieca, Tom Stack & Associates*; © Erich Hosking*
12–13: © Francisco Erize, Bruce Coleman Ltd.*; Jean Helmer
14–15: Trevor Boyer; Jean Helmer
16–17: Jean Helmer; © Martin Bruce, Tom Stack & Associates*
18–19: Jean Helmer; © Charles G. Summers Jr., Tom Stack & Associates*
20–21: Jean Helmer
22–23: © Roger Wilmshurst, Bruce Coleman Ltd.*
24–25: © Charlie Ott, Bruce Coleman Ltd.*; Jean Helmer
26–27: Patricia Wynne; © P. Berger, NAS*; Trevor Boyer
28–29: Peter Babakitis
30–31: © Ron Dillow, Tom Stack & Associates*
32–33: Patricia Wynne; © Robert T. Smith, Nature Photographers Ltd.*
34–35: Patricia Wynne; © Rod Planck, Tom Stack & Associates*
36–37: © John Shaw, Bruce Coleman Ltd.*; © Christian Zuber, Bruce Coleman Ltd.*
38–39: © Tom Stack, Tom Stack & Associates*; © Charles G. Summers Jr., Tom Stack & Associates*
40–41: © Phil & Loretta Hermann, Tom Stack & Associates*; Patricia Wynne
42–43: Patricia Wynne
44–45: © Norman Tomalin, Bruce Coleman Ltd.*; © John Shaw, Tom Stack & Associates*
46–51: Yoshi Miyake
52–53: Samantha Carol Smith
54–55: © Michael Gore, Nature Photographers Ltd.*; Yoshi Miyake
56–57: Samantha Carol Smith; © Leonard Lee Rue III, Bruce Coleman Ltd.*
58–59: Samantha Carol Smith
60–61: © S.C. Porter, Bruce Coleman Ltd.*
62–63: © Roger Wilmshurst, Bruce Coleman Ltd.*; Yoshi Miyake
64–65: © Derek Washington, Nature Photographers Ltd.*
66–67: © John Markham, Bruce Coleman Ltd.*; Harry McNaught; Arthur Singer; © H. Rivarola, Bruce Coleman Ltd.*
68–69: © Michael Gore, Nature Photographers Ltd.*; © Rod Planck, Tom Stack & Associates*
70–73: Heidi Palmer
74–75: Richard Hook
76–77: © Jen & Des Bartlett, Bruce Coleman Ltd.*

78–81: Richard Hook
82–83: © Jen & Des Bartlett, Bruce Coleman Ltd.*; © John Gerlach, Tom Stack & Associates*
84–85: © M.P. Kahl, Bruce Coleman Ltd.*
86–88: Richard Hook
89: © Francisco Erize, Bruce Coleman Ltd.*
90–91: Richard Hook
92–93: © David Hosking*
94–95: © John Markham, Bruce Coleman Ltd.*; Heidi Palmer
96–99: Richard Hook
100–101: © John Markham, Bruce Coleman Ltd.*; John Rignall; Trevor Boyer; © Carol Hughes, Bruce Coleman Ltd.*
102–103: © Adrian Davies, Bruce Coleman Ltd.*; © Wayne Lankinen, Bruce Coleman Ltd.*
104–109: Roberta Polfus
110–111: © Gregory A. Yovan, Tom Stack & Associates*
112–113: Nancy Lee Walter
114–115: Peter Babakitis; © Leonard Lee Rue III, Tom Stack & Associates*
116–118: © Leonard Lee Rue III, Bruce Coleman Ltd.*
119: Nancy Lee Walter
120–121: Roberta Polfus
122–123: © Jen & Des Bartlett, Bruce Coleman Ltd.*
124–125: © Wayne Lankinen, Bruce Coleman Ltd.*
126–127: Oxford Illustrators Ltd.
128–129: © Wayne Lankinen, Bruce Coleman Ltd.*
130–131: Nancy Lee Walter
132–133: Oxford Illustrators Ltd.; © Hans Reinhard, Bruce Coleman Ltd.*; John Rignall; Trevor Boyer
134–135: © M.P.L. Fogden, Bruce Coleman Ltd.*; © G.C. Kelley, Tom Stack & Associates*
136–139: Pamela Ford Johnson
140–141: © M.P. Kahl, Bruce Coleman Ltd.*
142–143: © Leonard Lee Rue III, Tom Stack & Associates*
144–145: © Christian Mundt, Tom Stack & Associates*
146–147: Patricia Wynne
148–149: © Jeff Foott, Bruce Coleman Ltd.*
150–151: © Peggy Heard, Nature Photographers Ltd.*; Pamela Ford Johnson
152–153: Patricia Wynne
154–157: © Gunter Zeisler, Bruce Coleman Ltd.*; Patricia Wynne
158–159: © Wayne Lankinen, Bruce Coleman Ltd.*
160–161: © Bruce Coleman*; © Richard Stacks, Dandelet Interlinks*; Patricia Wynne; Oxford Illustrators Ltd.
162–163: © G.D. Plage, Bruce Coleman Ltd.*; © Jeff Foott, Bruce Coleman Ltd.*
164–167: Yoshi Miyake
168–169: © W. Garst, Tom Stack & Associates*
170–171: Yoshi Miyake
172–173: Walter Linsenmaier
174–175: © Hans Reinhard, Bruce Coleman Ltd.*
176–178: Jean Helmer
179: © WWF/K. Weber, Bruce Coleman Ltd.*; John Rignall
180–181: © J.L. Mason, ARDEA*; © Erich & David Hosking*
182–186: Roberta Polfus
187: © John Mackinnen, Bruce Coleman Ltd.*
188–189: Richard Hook
190–191: © M.P. Harris, Bruce Coleman Ltd.*; Samantha Carol Smith
192–193: © Eric Crichton, Bruce Coleman Ltd.*
194–195: Samantha Carol Smith
196–197: © Steven Martin, Tom Stack & Associates*; © Alain Compost, Bruce Coleman Ltd.*
198–199: Richard Hook
200–201: Samantha Carol Smith; Roberta Polfus
202–204: Richard Hook
205: © Gunter Zeisler, Bruce Coleman Ltd.*
206–207: © Jen & Des Bartlett, Bruce Coleman Ltd.*; © James Hancock, Nature Photographers Ltd.*; © Steve Martin, Tom Stack & Associates*
208–209: Guy Tudor: John Rignall; Trevor Boyer; John Rignall; © Roy Williams, Bruce Coleman Ltd.*
210–211: © M.P. Kahl, Bruce Coleman Ltd.*; © G.C. Kelley, Tom Stack & Associates*
212–215: Pamela Ford Johnson
216–217: © F.S. Mitchell, Tom Stack & Associates*
218–219: © Jen & Des Bartlett, Bruce Coleman Ltd.*

Index

This index is an alphabetical list of the important things covered in both words and pictures in this book. The index shows you what page or pages each thing is on. For example, if you want to find out what the book tells about a particular subject, such as the emu, look under emu. You will find a group of words, called an entry, like this: **emu**, 77, *with picture*. This entry tells you that you can read about the emu on page 77. The words *with picture* tell you that there is a picture of an emu on this page, too. Sometimes, the book only tells you about a thing and does not show a picture. Then the words *with picture* will not be in the entry. It will look like this: **tailorbird**, 21. Sometimes, there is only a picture of a thing in the book. Then the word *picture* will appear before the page number, like this: **Indian Peacock**, *picture*, 27.

Cyclo-teacher® The easy-to-use learning system

Features hundreds of cycles from seven valuable learning areas

Here's how Cyclo-teacher works—in 3 easy steps!

Step 1—Asks a new question or poses a problem.

Step 2—Learner writes in answer or response.

Step 3—Learner checks his or her answer against correct response by flipping a lever.

Cyclo-teacher—the remarkable learning system based on the techniques of programmed instruction—comes right into your home to help stimulate and accelerate the learning of basic skills, concepts, and information. Housed in a specially designed file box are the Cyclo-teacher machine, Study Wheels, Answer Wheels, a Manual, a Contents and Instruction Card, and Achievement Record sheets.

Your child will find Cyclo-teacher to be a new and fascinating way to learn—much like playing a game. Only, Cyclo-teacher is much more than a game—it teaches new things

. . . reinforces learning . . . and challenges a youngster to go beyond!

Features hundreds of Study Cycles to meet the individual needs of students—your entire family—just as the *Childcraft Annual* is a valuable learning aid. And, best of all, lets you track your own progress—advance at your own pace! Cyclo-teacher is available by writing us at the address below:

The Childcraft Annual
Post Office Box 3822
Chicago, IL 60654

These beautiful bookstands—

specially designed to hold your entire program,
including *Childcraft Annuals*.

Height: 26-3/8''
with 4'' legs.
Width: 28-3/4''
Depth: 8-3/16''

Height: 8-3/4''
Width: 14-1/2''
Depth: 8''

Most parents like having a convenient place
to house their *Childcraft Annuals* and their
Childcraft library. A beautiful floor-model
bookstand —constructed of solid hardwood —is available in either walnut or
fruitwood finish.

You might prefer the attractive hardwood
table racks, also available in either walnut or
fruitwood finish. Let us know by writing us at
the following address:

The Childcraft Annual
Post Office Box 3822
Chicago, IL 60654